GREECE AND THE GRI

The 2023 Greece Travel Guide

Sara Black

Copyright

CONTENTS

WELCOME TO GREECE AND THE GREEK ISLAND

Greece offers exquisite scenery, more than 150 inhabited islands, more than 300 sunny days each year, and distinctive history. Greece is a wonderful place to travel all year round because of its great variety of morphology and climatic conditions. Get spoilt for choice with some of the most significant cultural heritage sites with breathtaking landscapes and some of the most beautiful islands in the world, a culture alive with emotive music, excellent cuisine, and adrenaline-pumping activities! The nation also provides top-notch travel options and services for every kind of traveler. Both children and families with kids will find it to be great.

10 Great Reasons to Visit Greece

1. Historical Monument

Greek culture is where Western culture first emerged. Where the first Olympians competed. Ascend stone-made steps to the monasteries of Meteora, which are perched above soaring rocks. Consider the oracle's guidance while admiring the magnificence of Delphi, taking in a play under the stars in a historic outdoor theater, and being astounded by enormous marble sculptures dragged up from the sea. Then discover provocative modern art, the gloomy pulse of rebetika, and artisans creating brand-new artwork using age-old methods. Greece is always pursuing new cultural endeavors, and its calendar is jam-packed with events like festivals and exhibitions.

2. Extraordinary Natural

No matter if you're a dedicated beach bum or a serious adrenaline junkie, Greece has something for you. Days pass by quickly in the perpetual sunshine and sea filled with islands that are bordered by beaches with white sand and pine trees providing shade. Get lost on clogged Byzantine routes, climb volcanoes, search for dolphins and sea turtles, and pedal through impenetrable woodlands. Get on a boat and sail off into the endless, brilliant blue. Wander through olive groves, charming towns, and verdant woodlands. Rock climbing and wreck diving locations offer breathtaking views for thrill-seekers.

3. Local Cuisine

Greek cuisine's signature dishes are well-known worldwide. Olive oil and feta are widely available nationwide. However, visiting here is a gourmet experience because of the distinctive regional cooking methods. Spices with flavors you've never experienced before, mountain greens, standard fare, and seafood direct from the sea are served. Risottos, pasta dishes, and soft desserts all feature Italian influences, as do Turkish sauces. Discover the revival of time-tested dishes with a contemporary twist.

4. Gorgeous Beaches

Greece provides beaches for every preference, including those with sand, pebbles, and rocks. With about 160,000 kilometers of coastline and 380 Blue Flag award-winning beaches, it is challenging to choose which are the best and most beautiful beaches in the nation. Each one has a certain beauty that makes it stand out from the others and ensures that the visitor will never forget it. Your every want will be satisfied in a paradise of pristine beaches and brilliantly warm blue waters.

5. The Mediterranean Climate

Despite Greece's relatively modest size, the country has a wide range of climates in its many areas. In contrast to the verdant Ionians, which are cooler and receive more rainfall, southern islands like Santorini may be extremely hot and dry. Snow can linger on some mountaintops through the summer, making high-altitude locations colder. Summers are generally sunny, warm, and dry. Snow can fall as far south as Athens on occasion during the winter months when temperatures fluctuate about 50 F (10 °C). October through March is the rainy season.

6. A Budget-Friendly Destination

In comparison to other well-known regions of Europe, Greece has long been renowned for its affordable prices. While it is true that Greece has many upscale and pricey businesses, it is still possible to travel throughout this fascinating nation on a shoestring budget. Beaches are open to everyone for free enjoyment, and traditional tavernas and kafeneia are reasonably priced.

7. Sensational Greek Islands

Every year, hundreds of thousands of people visit the stunning and unusual Greek islands. On the islands, you may find everything from stunning beaches to historic sites, vibrant harbors, and active volcanoes. One of the most beautiful islands in all of Greece, Santorini is unquestionably one of the top destinations.

Mykonos, another Cyclades Island, is a contemporary, cosmopolitan city with old-world whitewashed homes and winding lanes. In addition, the nightlife is one of the most well-liked activities worldwide.

The capital and largest island of the Dodecanese archipelago, Rhodes, is situated on the Aegean Sea coast. It is well-known for its broad sandy beaches and historical sites. One of the must-see islands is Corfu, which is far north of the Greek Ionian Islands.

8. Best family holiday destination

Greece is undoubtedly a paradise for people wishing to travel with their families. Some beaches allow you to completely unwind because there is zero risk there. There are nearly always coves that have been weathered by the wind and shallow, quiet waters.

White sand beaches that go on forever, like Elafonisi, seem to be there only for kids. Children will play for hours, learn to swim, or give bread to the fish. Little family paradises can be found in natural coves that are shielded from powerful seas.

Additionally, kids will like Greek food. Kids particularly enjoy treats like the tastiest homemade French fries, unusual types of cheese, and exquisite seasonal fruit.

9. Vibrant Nightlife

Greece has a thriving nightlife with activity all around. There are numerous fantastic places to go partying, including upscale bars where you may sip cocktails and dance until the sun comes up. The island of Mykonos, which has the best beach parties and nightclubs, is one of the most well-known locations for partying. So, if you love the nightlife, Greece is the perfect place for you.

10. Excellent hospitality

Greeks are known for their extraordinarily generous hospitality, which is unsuitable everywhere. When inviting people over, Greeks are very kind and giving; when they visit friends, they frequently bring cakes and wine as gifts. The word FILOTIMO, which stands for kindness and hospitality, is something that Greeks take great delight in. Greeks will always enjoy your presence; therefore, you'll experience the satisfaction of meeting them.

CHAPTER ONE

Top 20 Stunning Attractions in Greece

Greece has around 6,000 islands, all of which are embellished with a variety of pebbly and sandy beaches. Greece is one of Europe's top sun-and-sea vacation spots, but it's also the continent's cultural and historical superpower. The Acropolis alone is worth the flight miles because it is one of the most recognizable places on Earth.

1. Santorini

The largest island in the Santorini archipelago, which is comprised of several smaller islands, is called Santorini. It is situated in the Aegean Sea, south of the Greek mainland. It is a circular island with a lagoon in the middle that is extremely close to the South Aegean Volcanic Arc, a very active volcano. Extreme volcanic eruptions that occurred about 3600 years ago gave the area its odd geographic configuration today.

A beautiful landscape is created here by the white-washed homes and spectacular cities perched on the island's cliffs. It is best known for the layout of its cities, which have cobblestone streets and a combination of Venetian and Cycladic architecture.

Even more spectacular is the way the sun sets on the cliffs and the houses, which is reflected in the water below. Greek island Santorini is a destination that should not be missed.

2. Acropolis, Athens

The Acropolis of Athens, one of Greece's most revered locations, is an old citadel that still has the ruins of several old structures. These structures are most notable for their Parthenon, Propylaia, Erechtheion, and Athena Nike temple. These structures are all extremely important in terms of archeology and architecture, and nearly all of them were constructed in the fifth century, which is considered to be Greece's golden period. Today, the area operates as a museum and draws a ton of visitors who wish to experience the magnificent heritage of this great country.

3. Mykonos

Mykonos commonly referred to as the "island of the winds," is a Greek island that is very well-liked by visitors, particularly for its exotic nightlife. It is a legendary island with a long history. The legendary battle between Zeus and the Titans took place in Mykonos in Greek mythology, and it is supposed that Hercules the Great was murdered there. The 85 square kilometer island, which is home to some amazing clubs, bars, and restaurants in addition to its legendary stories, is a party paradise. Mykonos is sometimes likened to the Spanish island of Ibiza since it has beaches that are ideal for sunbathing and resting.

4. Acropolis Museum, Athens

One of the most popular tourist destinations in Athens is the Acropolis Museum. It is an ultra-modern glass and steel edifice with light and airy exhibition areas designed by Swiss architect Bernard Tschumi and constructed exclusively to display ancient artifacts from the Acropolis.

The top attractions in this area are the statue of a young man carrying a calf from the sixth century BC, the Caryatids, which are sculptures of female figures that supported the Erechtheion, and the contentious Parthenon Marbles. The cafe-restaurant terrace at the museum offers breathtaking views of the Acropolis.

5. Delphi

The sanctuary and oracle of Apollo were located in Delphi, which was once the most significant location in ancient Greek religion. Audience members could overlook the entire sanctuary as well as the breathtaking surroundings below thanks to the old theater of Delphi's hilltop location. It had 5,000 seats when it was first completed in the fourth century. It is currently among Greece's most popular tourist destinations.

6. Meteora

Another collection of magnificent Greek Orthodox monasteries can be found at Meteora, which is situated in the Pindus Mountains in central Greece next to the Pineios River. Six monasteries make up the complex, which is perched atop the mountain's natural sandstone pillars. These monasteries were first built in the fourteenth century. It was inhabited by a few highly virtuous hermit monks and remained off-limits to commoners for all of the recorded time. Only those who were the most inspired might find sanctuary here because of the way it was constructed.

7. Corfu

Off the mainland's western coast, in the Ionian Sea, is the Greek island of Corfu. The magnificent Italianate architecture of Corfu Town, the island's capital and longtime Venetian stronghold has earned its recognition as a UNESCO World Heritage Site. Explore its charming pedestrian-only alleyways to find two strongholds from the 16th century and the arcaded Liston, which is surrounded by vintage cafes.

The island is lush and lovely outside of the main town, with rough limestone cliffs plunging into the sea in its north and velvety green hills in its south. Paleokastritsa, on the west coast and about 25 kilometers from Corfu Town, is the beach located with the highest number of visitors. Here, several deep, curved bays hide pebble and sand beaches that extend into a crystal-clear sea. An airport and ferries from the Greek mainland's Igoumenitsa and Patras service Corfu.

8. Zákynthos

Another major tourist attraction in Greece is the island of Zákynthos (Zante), which boasts stunning beauty both above and below the sea. It is also conveniently positioned in the Ionian Sea, 16 kilometers off the west coast of the Peloponnese.

The spectacular sea caverns like the Blue Caves, which are off the island's northern tip, and the island's pebble and sand beaches, the most famous of which is Shipwrecthe k Beach, are two of its main draws. The walls of the cave take on a magnificent light as the glittering water inside reflects the hue of the blue sky. One of the many water-related attractions on this island is the Blue Caves. Scuba diving and snorkeling are also fantastic.

9. Mystras

Mystras, which is close to ancient Sparta and was ruled by ancestors of the Byzantine emperor in the 14th and 15th centuries, served as the Peloponnesus's capital. The location was occupied during the Ottoman era but was abandoned in 1832, leaving only the majestic medieval ruins, set in a stunning environment.

10. Samaria Gorge

On the island of Crete, the Samaria Gorge is located in the southwest of Greece. It is a valley that cuts through the White Mountains and was made by a river that formerly flowed through it. There was a small settlement in the gorge, but it was removed to create room for the national park. A very well-liked tourist activity supported by guides is a trek through the Samaria Gorge. The 16 km long gorge can be traversed in 4 to 7 hours, with its rugged cliffs and ancient cypress and pine trees. It is a section of the global biosphere reserve.

11. Rhodes Town

Rhodes is the biggest Dodecanese Island, and it is located in the Aegean Sea not far from Turkey. One of the major tourist locations in Greece is Rhodes Town, the nation's capital and a UNESCO World Heritage Site. With the help of the Knights of St. John, who acquired possession of the island in the 14th century, it is surrounded by a striking defense system that includes imposing towers and gates.

Walking around the old town's car-free cobblestone streets is a delight. Visitors can take an excursion boat to Marmaris on the Turkish coast, which is nearby, and the charming hillside seaside village of Lindo's. Additionally, to frequent ferries from Piraeus, the port in Athens, Rhodes has an airport.

12. Nafplio

Nafplio, frequently called the loveliest city in Greece, is a favorite weekend getaway location for affluent Athenians. In 1828, it became the first capital of modern Greece before Athens took control in 1834. It was built on a small peninsula on the east coast of the Peloponnese.

Spend an afternoon or a whole day exploring the old town, which is free of cars and home to majestic churches and mansions built in the Neoclassical style. The old town is also guarded by the Palamidi Fortress, which dates back to the 18th century. Tiryns, Epidaurus Theater, and Ancient Corinth are tourist destinations close by.

13. Myrtos Beach

Myrtos Beach, on the northwest coast of Kefalonia Island, has been named one of the most beautiful beaches in all of Europe by travelers. It has gained a place of great esteem among tourists from all over the world because of its stunning deep blue water with a tint of turquoise and the shore full of round, white cobblestone pebbles shining like diamonds. The beach is surrounded by many beautiful vistas as it lies in the shadows of the Agia Dynati and Kalon Oros mountains. It's the ideal place to spend some great moments in your life, and the lovely village of Divarata is only 2 kilometers away. So, this magnificent beach is unquestionably one of the most amazing Greece attractions.

14. Lindos

On the Greek island of Rhodes, the historic village of Lindos is comprised of a maze of cobblestone lanes surrounded by whitewashed homes. The Lindos Acropolis rises above the town and provides breathtaking views of the bays and shoreline in the area. The town core is not far from Lindos and Saint Paul's beaches.

15. Crete

One of the most popular holiday spots in Greece is the enormous island of Crete. The island is popular with tourists from throughout the world since it has some of Greece's best beaches. Some of Crete's most well-known beaches range in size from narrow arcs of sand surrounded by restaurants and promenades to expansive natural stretches lapped by crystal-clear waves and offering limitless vistas of the surrounding sea.

However, Crete is not just about the beaches. It includes a good number of noteworthy archeological sites, notably the magnificent Palace of Knossos, which is close to the lovely city of Heraklion. Both the laid-back village of Agios Nikolaos and the historic city of Chania offers lovely old shoreline sections that are ideal for spending long afternoons on a café terrace taking in the sights.

Avoid the larger towns and travel to the south coast of Crete's smaller settlements like Plakias or Matala for more secluded beaches and breathtaking mountain scenery.

16. Thessaloniki

Despite not being on many people's lists of places to visit, Thessaloniki doesn't seem to mind. The locals are content to be the only ones visiting the location and all of its attractions. The city's Byzantine churches, which are on the UNESCO World Heritage List, are the main sights to see, but there are also several Roman ruins (such as the Triumphal Arch of Galerius and the Rotunda from the fourth century), the White Tower on the seafront from the fifteenth century, and a top-notch Byzantine Museum that are worth visiting.

Thessaloniki, also known as Salonica, is the second-largest city in Greece after Athens and is located in the northern Aegean Sea. It was established in 316 BC and has always been a nexus of different cultures and religions because of its location close to both Bulgaria and Turkey. The highest mountain in Greece, Mount Olympus, is a popular destination for day trips from Thessaloniki. This stunning natural sight is only 80 kilometers away and is easily accessible via good roads. From Prionia's vicinity, the most well-known hiking trails start.

17. Corinth Canal

Be sure to stop at the overlook above the Corinth Canal as you approach the Peloponnese Peninsula while driving along the rather level Highway 8. It was only in 1883 that this canal, which had been envisioned and attempted as early as 1 CE, was completed. Unfortunately, the canal never proved to be very popular or financially beneficial for its builders. Consider how the ancient builders were able to drill down through the solid rock to carve out the canal as you leave your car parked and step out onto the bridge.

18. Palace of Knossos

When visiting Crete, you must see the Palace of Knossos, one of the most important archeological sites in all of Greece. The site was extensively repaired and is believed to date back to the Late Minoan period. As with many Greek archeological sites, some parts of this location take considerable imagination, even though the standing buildings give you a clear idea of how previously they appeared. The layout of the complex is excellent, with walkways circling the main structures and public spaces.

The major structures at the walkway's end have some vibrant paintings on them, so be sure to look them over. Near Heraklion, one of the main entrances to Crete, is where you can find the Palace of Knossos. It's simple to schedule tours.

19. Mycenae

One of the most important archeological sites south of Athens is the majestic citadel of Mycenae, which is highly recommended for anybody with an interest in Greek history. Mycenae, the pinnacle of the Mycenaean civilization, is a spectacular hilltop city that dates back to roughly 1350 BCE. The majestic Lion Gate is one of Mycenae's most notable sights. The gate is made of precisely arranged stones over a rectangular gateway and is set into the slope of the hill. The renowned gold mask was discovered here by the explorer Heinrich Schliemann in the late 19th century. Step inside the beautifully dome-shaped Treasury of Atreus to gain some relief from the sun.

20. Cape Sounion

Cape Sounion, home to the Temple of Poseidon, is situated at the southernmost point of Attica at the tip of the Sounio Peninsula. The building was made completely of white marble and dedicated to Poseidon in 5 BC. One of the most well-known buildings from Athens' Golden Age is the Temple of Poseidon. Three sides of the temple face the Aegean Sea, and viewing the sunset over the water from this vantage point is breathtaking. 34 columns made up the Poseidon Temple. There are now only 15 people left. The name Lord Byron can be seen if you pay close attention to one of the columns. During a visit to the historical location in 1810, the well-known poet wrote his name.

Best Greek islands to visit

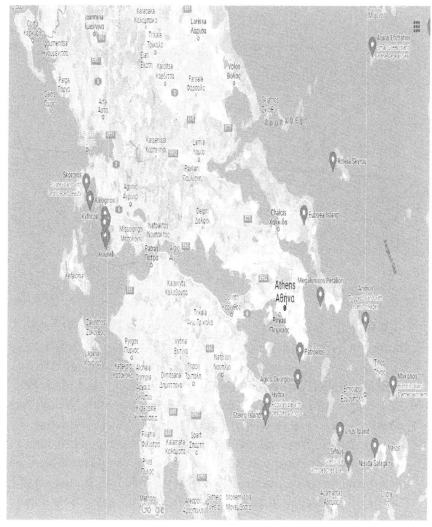

Crete

Crete, the largest island in Greece, essentially meets all criteria. It offers accommodations ranging from boutique hotels to all-inclusive resorts with sports facilities and kids' clubs. It also features sand beaches, rugged mountains, and myth-filled archaeological sites. Its southern location offers it the longest summer of any Greek island as well as some of the hottest winters in all of Europe. There are beaches to accommodate any sun seeker, as well as mountains and gorges for outdoor activities and the palace at Knossos for history aficionados. The coastlines range from populated seafronts to unspoiled coves.

The Asterion Suites & Spa offers the best of both worlds: a boutique retreat with design-driven suites and a superb Cretan restaurant that is close to old Chania and touristy Platanias with its shops, bars, and restaurants.

Where to stay in Crete:

- **For families: Domes Zeen Chania and Cretan Malia Park**
- **For romance: Acros Wellness Suites**
- **For a great location: Blue Palace Resort & Spa**

- **For a village stay: Kapsaliana Village**
- **For a private stay: Azure Awe**
- **For a group: Cien sleeps 16 people**

Skiathos

In terms of beach chic, Skiathos pulls its weight. This region, which is home to some of Greece's most picturesque beaches, is where bottle-green pines, which provide natural shade for bohemian days by the sea, descend from the steep interior to meet the Aegean. Big Banana, Little Banana, Ampelakia, and the famed Koukounaries are four of the island's nicest beaches, while Elivi Skiathos is a luxurious hideaway that makes a great spot to stay. Make things interesting by taking excursions into Skiathos Town, where upscale eateries and drink bars with harbor views provide the setting for exciting street celebrations almost every summer night.

Where to stay in Skiathos:

- **For a hotel stay: Elivi Skiathos**
- **For a private stay: Villa Azalea**

Corfu

One of the greenest islands in Greece is Corfu. This Ionian Island has approximately 60 breathtaking beaches and secret coves sprinkled throughout it, in addition to its steep slopes covered with olive trees, pencil-thin cypresses, and 400 different species of wildflowers. Try the wilder Rovinia, which is only accessible by boat or on foot. Dassia and Kontokali are popular destinations for family vacations. Corfu Town's eclectic mix of Venetian, British, French, and Greek architecture, history, and gastronomy is the perfect place to satisfy your need for culture.

Where to stay in Corfu:

- For a standout spa: **Angsana Corfu Resort & Spa**
- For all-inclusive: **Ikos Dassia**
- For romance: **Domes Miramare**
- For families: **Domes of Corfu**
- For groups: **Emerald Oasis sleeps 10 people**

Rhodes

The ideal Greek island for families is without a doubt, Rhodes. This was the island of the sun god Helios, whose statue (the Colossus of Rhodes) was one of the Seven Wonders of the Ancient World, in addition to quiet beaches offering safe swimming, there are plenty of days away from the sand. Rhodes Town, one of Greece's most evocative island capitals, has the imprint of Roman, Ottoman, and Venetian occupations.

Where to stay in Rhodes:

- **For romance: Casa Cook**
- **For history: Kókkini Porta Rossa**
- **For a boutique stay: Melenos Art Boutique Hotel**

Mykonos

Brigitte Bardot, Grace Kelly, and — perhaps most famously — Jackie Onassis all took vacations in Mykonos in the 1960s, making it the Aegean's premier destination for the jet set. Nowadays' high rollers spend their money at pricey beach clubs like Nammos and Scorpios, but if that's not your style, there are plenty of places where the lunch bill won't make your eyes wet. The Semeli Hotel, a posh getaway with fine food, helpful service, and a nice pool that is only a 10-minute walk from the waterfront and its iconic windmills, is located in Mykonos Town, which is stunning in the evening.

Where to stay in Mykonos:

- **For romance: Cali Mykonos**
- **For the party scene: Soho Roc House**
- **For a laidback stay: Once in Mykonos**
- **For families: Santa Marina resort**
- **For groups: Bluewave XL sleeps 36 people**

Naxos

Naxos is the largest of the Cyclades islands and one of the least visited, so it has quiet sandy beaches and a low-key, relaxed attitude distinct from its crowded neighbors. This island, which packs a lot of variation into a compact area, allows visitors to escape the madding throngs of tourists by relaxing on an unending series of silky sand beaches or hiking up into remote mountain settlements.

Where to stay in Naxos:

- **For romance: Naxian on the Beach**
- **For laidback luxury: Kavos**
- **For a private stay: Eye of Naxos Sky**
- **For families: Hidden Hill**

Zante

The island of Zakynthos, also known as Zante, is a popular party destination thanks to its infamous Laganas nightlife district, but this sun-drenched Ionian Isle, also referred to by the Venetians as "the flower of the East," is also home to some of the most breathtaking natural beauty in the Mediterranean. This includes the magnificent Shipwreck Beach, whose turquoise waters are enclosed by towering white cliffs and can only be accessed by boat, as well as Zakynthos Marine Park, which is home to cunning turtles and slippery seals.

Where to stay in Zante:

- **For families: Porto Zante**
- **For romance: Zante Maris Suites and Olea All Suite Hotel**
- **For a private stay: Halcyon Seas**
- **For a group: Ble Kyma sleeps 12 people**

34

Symi

This rocky Dodecanese Island, which formerly housed boat builders, merchants, and sponge divers, was the richest in the archipelago. Just a tenth of its 19ᵗʰ-century population still resides there now, although the population grows as day visitors arrive by ferry from Rhodes, a nearby island. Peace returns as they leave, save for the giggling and clinking of drinks on the Gialos waterfront and the upper village of Chorio, whose maze of winding alleyways was built to confuse sea pirates. The horseshoe harbor and sorbet-colored neoclassical structures in Symi are magnificent. One of these mansions has been transformed into the 1900 Hotel, which boasts a retro aesthetic and a cozy atmosphere that feels like they belong in another time.

Where to stay in Symi:

- **For a hotel stay: The Old Markets**
- **For a private stay: On The Rocks**

Skopelos

The pebble beaches of Skopelos are ideal if you don't like sand getting into your belongings even though it may be more comfortable to lay on. Even better, the absence of sand leaves the sea pristine and turquoise, making for wonderfully unforgettable dips. The island is thrilling for its two red-roofed settlements, Skopelos Town and Glossa, and an interior that is emerald with trees, despite being most known as the location for the film Mamma Mia!

Kefalonia

Kefalonia is one of the top Greek islands to visit because it is home to Myrtos Beach and the site for Captain Corelli's Mandolin. Aside from relaxing days spent at its crowded beach resorts or restful villas tucked away in the countryside, there are wrecked villages to visit (a relic of the 1953 earthquake) and, in Argostoli, the chance to see loggerhead turtles swimming in the harbor. The laid-back pace of island life is conducive to soothing getaways, and F Zeen Retreat, an exclusive retreat for adults with a spa, outdoor theater, and private beach, embodies this philosophy to a tee.

Where to stay in Kefalonia:

- **For an adult-only retreat: F Zeen**
- **For families: Emelisse Nature Resort**
- **For groups: Odyssea sleeps 12 people**
- **For a private stay: Wilderness Whisperings house**
- **For something unique: This sky-high villa**

Sifnos

Sifnos, known as the "Greek Island of Gastronomy," has long been a haven for foodies who savor dishes like mastelo lamb marinated in red wine and herbs or chickpea croquettes baked in locally made crocks. Nikalaos Tselementes, who wrote the first Greek cookbook here in 1910, is often credited with coining the phrase. But this undiscovered island offers more than simply eating; you can climb to the medieval village of Kastro, shop in the capital Apollonia's chic boutiques, or visit one of the many ceramic studios to experience Sifnos' distinctive flavor.

Where to stay in Sifnos:

- **For romance: NÓS**
- **For a boutique stay: Verina Astra**
- **For families: Verina Terra**
- **For a laidback stay: Sifnos House**
- **For something unique: This windmill Airbnb**

Hydra

This charming island, which is accessible by ferry from Piraeus in Athens for an hour, enjoys complete peace due to a total restriction on cars and motorcycles. Since Leonard Cohen first arrived to play here in the 1960s, Hydra has been a gathering place for artists thanks to its attractive cobblestones, eye-catching architecture, and mules for transportation. Today, they visit the island to peruse the art galleries and take sea taxis to the blissfully undiscovered beach coves.

Where to stay in Hydra:

- **For a boutique stay: Orloff Boutique Hotel**
- **For a beachfront stay: Anemos**
- **For a group: Mirkella sleeps 12 people**

Santorini

Santorini is without a doubt the Greek island that comes to mind when you think of it. The largest of the Cyclades' mini-islands, Santorini features the stereotypically Greek whitewashed buildings, but its two main towns—blue-domed Oia and the capital Fira—perched precariously on the cliffs above a submerged volcano—offer some of the best views in the Mediterranean.

Santorini is a volcanic island, making it one of the most expensive in Greece and a veritable playground for the rich and famous. Despite this, you don't need much time there to enjoy its allure. The world-famous sunsets and world-class wineries make it something you simply must cross off your bucket list.

You can spend all day in Santorini's opulent boutiques, stroll along the cliffs of the caldera, and relax on the beaches with white, black, and red volcanic sand. You can ride a mule or a cable car up the 588 zigzagging steps if you arrive by sea. The cable car can be accessed from the port.

Where to stay in Santorini:

- **For laidback luxury: Perivolas**
- **For glamour: Nobu Hotel**
- **For romance: Andronis Boutique Hotel**
- **For families: The Vasilicos**
- **For groups: Elilia Superior Villa sleeps 8 people**
- **For something unique: this cave house**

Paros

Less than three hours away from Athens is the typical Cycladic island of Paros, with its fishing villages providing a typical Greek getaway. Paros is known as a party island, with a variety of cocktail bars and restaurants; you won't have trouble finding a happy hour here. Its typical Greek architecture is encircled in purple and red bougainvillea. There is more to do in Paros than just go out at night, though that is undoubtedly a draw. In addition, the island is a well-liked location for outdoor pursuits like scuba diving, horseback riding, windsurfing, and kitesurfing.

Visit Parikia, the island's capital, to see its whitewashed structures, villas in the Venetian style, historic monasteries, and blue church domes. Other places worth visiting include the satellite island of Antaparos with its stalagmite-filled caves and the port city of Náoussa, which served as Lefkes's former capital. Highlights include the archaeological museum, the yii Anárgyiri monastery, and the Ekatondapylian (previously the Katopoliani) church, one of the most impressive in the Aegean.

Where to Stay in Paxos:

- **For an authentic stay: Paxos Villa**
- **For a great location: Oneiro**

- **For groups: Panayia View sleeps 14 people**

Milos

Milos, which is situated just above the Sea of Crete and has more beaches than any other Cyclades Island combined, is undoubtedly one of Greece's best-kept secrets. Considering Milos' reasonable distance from Athens, a flight is preferable unless you don't mind waiting the extra seven hours it takes to travel there by ferry. The volcanic island of Milos has a long history of mining that dates back to the Neolithic era. It is renowned for its stunning natural scenery, which includes dramatic rock formations, hot springs, steam vents, and mineral quarries.

Where to stay on Milos:

- **For romance: Milos Cove**
- **For families: Captain Zeppos**
- **For an eco-retreat: Skinopi Lodge**
- **For an authentic stay: Achinos by The Sea**

Serifos

Located in the western Cyclades, Serifos is a small island that offers all the benefits of a remote Greek vacation without the tourist hordes: undeveloped, secluded beaches, wonderful walking paths, and top-notch tavernas. The views are also spectacular. A normally barren hilltop is dotted with hundreds of Greek Orthodox churches, ancient monasteries, and Cycladic structures that descend to the rocky coastline below. Today, Serifos is primarily known for its hilltop capital and a few abandoned mining trails despite once being a bustling mining hub. For a breathtaking view of this largely untamed island, climb up to Hora, also known as the Chora, the Greek term for an island's main town.

Where to stay on Serifos:

- **For a boutique stay: Verina Astra**
- **For romance: Chill & Co.**
- **For groups: Lenia sleeps 12 people**
- **For something unique: This 19th-century captain's house**

The Best Athens Museums

Acropolis Museum

One of the newest and best museums in Athens is the Acropolis Museum, which opened its doors in 2009. The museum is a light-filled exhibition space for artifacts from the Acropolis complex just next door, but it is also an archaeological site in and of itself, perched over a bygone Athenian neighborhood and equipped with glass floors that allow visitors to observe the dig below. Archaeologists are available to assist visitors and there are three floors of permanent collections, film presentations, and other exhibits. Moreover, the Parthenon is surrounded by a top-notch gift shop and a café/restaurant with a patio outside. combined well with a trip to the nearby Acropolis ancient site.

National Archaeological Museum

The first, best, and biggest archaeological museum in Greece, with a permanent collection of more than 11,000 pieces of ancient Greek art and artifacts from the Neolithic to late antiquity. Grecophiles, history enthusiasts, and museum lovers may all easily spend the day here, stopping at the cafe/restaurant right outside the main entrance to refuel.

Byzantine & Christian Museum

The largest collection of Byzantine artworks from the third to the twenty-first centuries can be seen in this museum, which was founded in 1914 and is situated in a palace designed in the Florentine style. Rare and well-preserved artifacts provide insight into the impact and legacy of the Byzantine Empire. Rare icons from the 13th century, including a mosaic of the Virgin Mary from Constantinople, as well as scriptures, frescoes, coins, and other artifacts, are on show. 900 meters east of Syntagma Square, near the Athens War Museum, with a cafe/restaurant and museum store on the property.

Museum of Cycladic Art

An excellent and family-friendly museum that originally belonged to the Greek shipping family of Dolly and Nikolaos Goulandris and now houses one of the largest private collections of Cycladic and Ancient Greek art in the world. The permanent collection, which spans four floors in a lovely Neo-classical palace from 1895, comprises Cycladic, Ancient Greek, and Cypriot art, as well as multimedia, shows that show scenes from the daily lives of Ancient Greeks (weddings, the birth of a baby, education, physical training, and more)

National Historical Museum

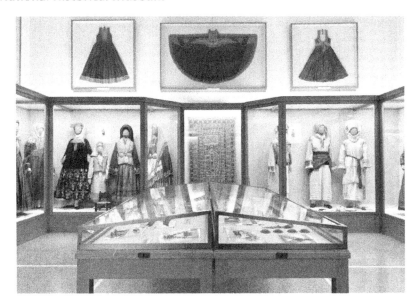

The permanent collection of the National Historical Museum in Athens, founded in 1882, tells the story of Greek culture throughout the ages through memorabilia and personal items from notable historical figures, classical paintings, genuine manuscripts, and a sizable collection of traditional Greek clothing and jewelry from various parts of Greece. One block northwest of Syntagma Square, it's all situated in the imposing structure that served as the Greek Parliament's home from 1875 to 1932.

Athens War Museum

This military-run museum, which was established in 1975 and pays tribute to everyone who fought for Greece's freedom, is a must-see for fans of history, the military, and aviation. Exhibits are arranged across two levels and take you through the history of Greek conflicts from antiquity to the present. These wars are brought to life through images, full uniforms, personal letters, artifacts, weaponry, and armor. Aerial displays of huge artillery pieces and engaging documentary films are outside the museum. A visit to the War Museum would go well with seeing the changing of the guard at the Hellenic Parliament, which is around 900 meters to the east of Syntagma Square.

The Paul and Alexandra Canellopoulos Museum

Paul and Alexandra Canellopoulos, prominent art collectors and businesspeople from the early to mid-20th century bequeathed an impressive private collection of antiquated artwork and antiques to the Greek government. The permanent collection includes artifacts dating from the Prehistoric to the Modern era, including figurines, busts, jewelry, weapons, coins, inscriptions, stone and clay vases, and more. These artifacts range in date from 3000-1200 BC to the 18th and 19th centuries AD. situated next to the Monastiraki metro stop in Plaka, in a neoclassical mansion built in 1864.

In 2007, this wonderful museum of modern art opened its doors to the public to showcase Greek artists both domestically and abroad. The museum houses a permanent collection of works by the renowned modern Greek painter Spyros Papaloukas in addition to revolving temporary exhibitions. Check the website for a current calendar of activities. The foundation also sponsors concerts, workshops, and educational programs for kids and adults at the museum. The structure has a fantastic gift shop on the ground floor and a Mediterranean restaurant with views of the National Garden and the Parliament Building on the first floor.

Athens City Museum

Two Neo-classical aristocratic residences from the 19th century that were originally owned by the Vouros and Eftaxias families now make up a small yet charming museum. The first royal family of Greece, King Otto, and Queen Amalia lived in the elder of the two homes, commonly known as the Old Residence, between 1836 and 1842 before relocating to their new palace in the current Parliament building. The tale of opulent Athens in the 1800s, when the city became Greece's capital following the War of Independence, is revealed through furnishings and personal items as well as engaging digital exhibitions.

Museum of Greek Folk Musical Instruments

A charming collection of more than 1,200 Greek folk musical instruments, dating from the 18th century to the present, is kept inside a 19th-century home next to the Roman Agora. Three floors of instruments are arranged according to type, and visitors can hear them in use through movies and headphones. During the summer, musical events are frequently given in the garden courtyard and there is a fantastic little museum store on site.

Kotsanas Museum of Ancient Greek Technology

A permanent collection of over 100 reconstructed Greek inventions from the year 2000 B.C. to the fall of the Ancient Greek world (323 B.C.) is on display at this interactive, family-friendly museum. These include operational replicas of ancient hydraulic technology, steam engines, medical technology, and more. There's even a replica of the Antikythera mechanism, which is thought to be the first computer in history. Ancient musical instruments and toys, as well as armor and weapons, are two more on-site displays that may be seen at the museum for a fee.

Museum of Modern Greek Culture

The Museum of Modern Greek Culture, established in 1918, has undergone several name changes and relocations throughout the years. It is currently awaiting the move to its new, permanent location across from the Hadrian's Library archeological site. The museum's temporary home, a stunning two-story historic mansion in Plaka with views of the Acropolis, offers several exhibits including objects from its sizable collection, themed around themes of the modern Greek experience.

The Benizelos Mansion

Built during the 16th and 17th centuries, the Benizelos Mansion is the oldest surviving home in Athens. Visits to this two-story home, which was once inhabited by Angelos Benizelos and his wife Syrigi Palaiologina, provide insight into the customs and way of life of Athens' aristocracy in the years leading up to the Greek revolution. Revoula, the couple's daughter, was a well-known humanitarian who worked to rescue Greek women who had been captured by the Ottomans and forced into harems. The Benizelos Mansion is sometimes referred to as the House of Saint Philothei in her honor because she was eventually declared a saint and given the name "Saint Philothei." The saint Philothei's remains are interred nearby in the Metropolitan Cathedral of Athens, which is close to the palace in Plaka.

The House on Panos Street: Man, and Tools Museum

A section of the Museum of Modern Greek Culture showcases primitive equipment and byproducts of manual labor as well as portrays Greek working life, primarily from the end of the War of Independence until the middle of the 20th century. It is a little museum in Plaka that is well worth a fast trip; through private collections and engaging exhibitions, visitors get a feel of what ordinary life would have been like and how far the industrial world has come.

Bathhouse of the Winds

This historic bathhouse, also known as the Hammam of Abid Efendi, was constructed during the Ottoman Empire (1453-1669) and used until 1956 as an annex of the Museum of Modern Greek Culture. It is Athens' lone remaining public bathhouse.

In Greece during the Ottoman Period, public hammams like this were an essential part of daily life. Bathhouses provided a place for social interaction, meditation, relaxation, and an escape from the daily grind in addition to being clean. These were the only areas outside of the home where women were permitted to go.

Goulandris Natural History Museum

The Goulandris Museum was the nation of Greece's first natural history institution, and it is situated in the northeastern suburb of Kifisia. In 1977, it grew to include biology, paleontology, and geology after being formed as a botanical museum to learn about and investigate Greek flora. Insects, mammals, birds, reptiles, shells, rocks, minerals, and fossils are all part of its permanent exhibit, along with species from Africa, North America, and Greece. This place also hosts transient exhibits. An on-site gift shop and café make this place very family-friendly.

Beaches in Greece

Myrtos Beach, Kefalonia

Best for Nature Enthusiasts

One of Greece's most stunning beaches is Myrtos Beach on the island of Kefalonia. Its stunning, deep-blue waters with flawless clarity are of extraordinary beauty.

Myrtos Beach is located on the island of Kefalonia, which is a member of the Ionian group of islands in the west of the nation, in the Pylaros district. On the island's northwestern side, it is situated between two mountains. Myrtos Beach is a multi-awarded beach that has been included in lists of the best beaches in the world for more than ten years running.

The Blue Flag, one of the most recognizable eco-labels in the world given to marinas and beaches that meet and maintain the highest environmental, sustainability, and safety standards, is given to Myrtos Beach each year. The fact that the water grows deep just a few steps from the shore is one of the unique features of Myrtos Beach.

Voidokilia Beach, Messinia

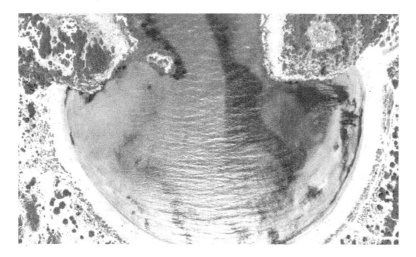

Best for Families

One of Greece's most exquisite beaches is Voidokilia Beach. It is situated on the Peloponnese peninsula in the Messinia region, only approximately 3 kilometers from Pylos town, one of Greece's most beautiful and ancient cities.

Beautiful lake Voidokilia has a distinctive shape. The beach is shielded from winds and waves due to its rounded shape. Since the water is shallow, even young children can readily swim there. Enjoy the long, sandy beach and climb to Nestor's Castle for a breathtaking view of the Ionian Sea. Be careful to bring water with you because there are no beach bars or sun loungers. Three things you must have been an umbrella, a hat, and sunscreen.

Agios Georgios Beach, Naxos

Agios Georgios, a Blue Flag beach, consistently ranks at the top of lists of the most family-friendly beaches in Greece. Naxos is known for its white, powdery sand beaches.

It is bordered by clear, shallow waters that are shielded from the winds, and it is only a short stroll from Naxos Town, the port, and some of the top hotels on the island. The younger youngsters can splash around while the older ones can engage in a range of beach activities. At the southern end, there is a water sports facility, and there are a lot of beach clubs and taverns there as well.

Elafonisi Beach, Crete

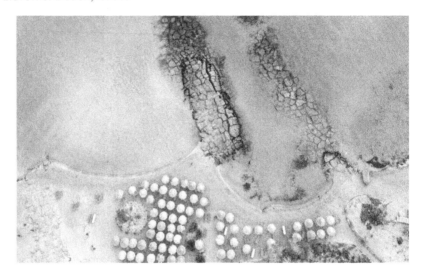

The island of Crete is the meeting place for gastronomy, culture, and authenticity. The Greek Island of Crete is home to some of the most incredible beaches in the world. It is really necessary to try Elafonisi, which is one of them.

The distinctive and magnificent Elafonisi lagoon is known for its pink sand, which is crushed shells in several areas. 76 kilometers separate from Chania town, which is located in the same region. No matter what time of day you visit the beach, it is perfect for swimmers of all abilities due to the water's relative shallowness and safety as well as the bay's protection from ferocious winds and large waves. A protected area under Natura 2000, it.

Simos Beach, Elafonisos

Simos Beach is one of the most well-known beaches in the Peloponnese and unquestionably a destination unto itself when it comes to summer vacations in Greece. If you enjoy the fine sand, the golden dunes, the crystal clear, translucent waters, and the breathtaking scenery, you are at the correct location. This magnificent beach, which is just a short drive—only 3 km—away from the major village of Elafonisos, Skala, is adored by both locals and tourists alike. It will take you around 3,5 hours to drive here from Athens. Once you arrive, you can either drive to the beach or arrive by boat that you can rent in Skala village.

The nights with a full moon are particularly special; it is worthwhile to remain out until late in the evening to witness the moon rise and the light shows that arise as reflections on the sea. If you're fortunate enough to be here, the August full moon is a must.

All types of swimmers, including young children, will find the swimming conditions to their liking. The beach is divided among areas that have been organized with sun loungers and umbrellas and areas that are free for you to choose your spot in the sun.

Sarakiniko Beach, Milos

Sarakiniko, on the north shore of Milos, has a lunar-like environment that gives it the appearance of being on another planet or possibly being made for a science fiction movie. It is encircled by the sea that ranges in color from pale sapphire to emerald green. You'll want to take pictures of the strange rocks that the wind and water have sculpted through time and perhaps bask in the sun on the white, smooth volcanic rocks in between cool dips. Don't forget your water bottle because there are no facilities of any type here; this is a location for adventurers to explore nature.

Super Paradise Beach, Mykonos

From Platis Gialos in Mykonos Town, you may take a taxi, a water taxi, or a bus to Super Paradise with ease.

It is the center of the island's well-known party scene and is known for its upscale beaches bars and clubs like Jackie O, lovely sandy sands, and turquoise waters for enjoying a variety of water sports. There are lots of umbrellas and sunbeds available so visitors can enjoy the sun between dips in the tempting sea.

Balos Beach, Crete

Balos is one of Crete's most beautiful and frequently photographed beaches. It can only be reached by boat or by driving a rough road to the trailhead and then taking a 20-minute climb. When no other people are around, arrive early to enjoy swimming in the transparent turquoise waters surrounding pristine white sand and stretches of pink. It feels like swimming in a large, warm natural pool while being shielded from the breeze. Even nobility, like Prince Charles and Princess Diana, have been drawn to it by its unique, wild beauty. Umbrellas, lounge chairs, and refreshments are available if you want to stay for the day.

Porto Katsiki, Lefkada

Best for Active Travelers

Greek for "Porto Goat," Porto Katsiki is so named because of the longer, more strenuous descent required to reach this long, sandy beach on Lefkada island. Despite its amusing moniker, it is undoubtedly one of Greece's most magnificent beaches. The hues of the ocean are unparalleled. Dramatic scenery, smooth, white beach, and turquoise waters. Once you see this beach, it will instantly become one of your top and favorite spots in the world.

About 40 kilometers separate Porto Katsiki from Lefkada's main town. You can travel here by car or, if you're lucky, by boat. Even in August, the Ionian Sea provides ideal sailing weather, and if you are aboard a sailing boat, you will have the chance to view shorelines that are inaccessible by automobile.

It is worthwhile to visit Lefkada Island any time between early May and late September or perhaps early October because it has the most beautiful waters and shores in all of Greece.

Papafragas Beach, Milos

Papafragas is a challenging beach to get to but it's worth the effort. It's located at the northernmost point of Milos and is only a 5-minute drive from Pollonia. You'll find a lovely beach encircled by high cliffs and natural caves by following the short path and descending a set of rickety-looking steps carved into the cliffside. It appears just like a dazzling, aquamarine-hued swimming pool from the top of the rock.

CHAPTER TWO
Need To Know

Location: Southern Europe, bordering Albania 282 km, Bulgaria 494 km, Turkey 206 km, The Former Yugoslav Republic of Macedonia 246 km

Capital: Athens

Climate: mostly mountains with ranges extending into the sea as peninsulas or chains of islands

Population: 11.1 million (2019 est.)

Ethnic Make-up: Greek 98%, other 2%

Religions: Greek Orthodox 98%, Muslim 1.3%, other 0.7%

Government: parliamentary republic; monarchy rejected by referendum 8 December 1974

Best time to visit Greece

Greece's best island-hopping season lasts from late September to early October, and many Greeks take advantage of it. The days are still long and pleasant, there are fewer people about, and the sea is at a perfect temperature. Just beware of those annoying dry northern winds (Meltemi), which can pick up around that time and jeopardize outdoor meals and beach activities (unless you're a windsurfer). While the waves are choppy, May to mid-June is also fantastic for avoiding crowds and peak pricing. Ferries to farther-flung islands run more often in July and August, whereas most Greek islands close for the winter months from November to March.

The Best Months to Visit Greece

- Best Time to Visit Mykonos: June to September
- Best Time to Visit Santorini: April, May, June, September, October, early November

- Best Time to Visit Crete: June and September
- Best Time to Visit Rhodes: June and September
- Best Time to Visit Naxos: June to September
- Best Time to Visit Paros: June to September
- Best Time to Visit Ios: July and August
- Best Time to Visit Athens: April, May, October, and November
- Best Time to Visit Corfu: June, July, and September
- Best Time to Visit Nafplio & Peloponnese: June and September

The Greek Islands – Where to Go

Greek Islands weather in January: cool with overcast skies and lots of rain.

Crete and Santorini are the best Greek islands to visit in January.

Greek Islands weather in February: chilly with overcast skies and lots of rain.

Crete and Santorini are the best Greek islands to visit in February.

Greek Islands weather in March: Some lovely bright days, some dreary, cold days, and moderate rain.

Crete, Santorini, and Rhodes are the three best Greek Islands to visit in March.

Greek Islands weather in April: Warm sunny days are typical, but not exactly swimming weather and minimal rain.

The best Greek islands to visit in April include Crete, Santorini, Rhodes, Corfu, Naxos, and Paros.

Greek Islands weather in May: Warm sunny days with a decent likelihood of beach weather, and little rain.

The best Greek islands to visit in May are Crete, Santorini, Rhodes, Kos, Corfu, Naxos, Paros, and Mykonos.

Greek Islands Weather in June: Days with high temperatures and little to no rain.

The best Greek islands to visit in June are all fantastic.

Greek Islands weather in July: Days with high temperatures and little to no rain.

Best Greek Islands to Visit in July: Greece's islands are all fantastic (but busy).

Greek Islands weather in August: Days with high temperatures and little to no rain.

The best Greek Islands to Visit in August are all fantastic (but busy).

Greek Islands Weather in September: Days with high temperatures and little to no rain.

The best Greek Islands to Visit in September are all fantastic.

Greek Islands weather in October: Few rainy days, warm sunny days with a decent likelihood of beach weather.

The best Greek islands to visit in October are Crete, Santorini, Rhodes, Kos, Corfu, Naxos, Paros, and Mykonos.

Greek Islands weather in November: A few lovely sunny days, a few gloomy, chilly days, and some light rain.

The best Greek islands to visit in November include Crete, Santorini, Naxos, Paros, and Rhodes.

Greek Islands in December: Cool with an overcast sky and lots of rain.

Santorini and Crete are the ideal Greek Islands to visit in December.

The Best time to visit Greece and the Greek Islands

Best Time to Visit the Greek Islands

For swimming, tanning, and beach weather, the Greek islands are at their finest from late May to early October. From April to early November, the islands are greatest for sightseeing, trekking, and exploring. The weather patterns in the Greek islands should be taken into account while planning a trip to Greece.

Best Time to Visit Athens

All seasons are great to visit Athens. Winter is a fantastic season to visit Athens because of the mild weather and lower tourist numbers. Although it is hot during the summer, there is always blue sky, little to no rain, and tables and chairs from bars and restaurants lined the sidewalks. The best seasons are spring and fall because of the pleasant weather, fewer visitors, and the lively environment.

Best Time to Visit Greece for Good Weather

Greece and the Greek islands experience their warmest weather from late May and early October when it is sunny and pleasant, and the water is suitable for swimming. Summer months see an increase in water temperature. In May, the waters will be suitable for swimming (even though the weather can be beautiful). In early September and August, the water is at its hottest. It is frequently feasible to swim between early May and late October, but this cannot be guaranteed.

Best Time to Visit Greek Beaches

The best months to visit Greece are July, August, and September if you want to enjoy lounging on the greatest beaches and swimming in the sea. However, the second half of September may still be ideal because many tourists are heading home and the sea is still comfortably warm from all the summer sun.

Best Time for Sightseeing

The best months for touring in Greece are often April through approximately mid-May, or October and into early November when there will be fewer people to obstruct the vistas and the weather is regularly pretty moderate; ideal for walking, but typically a touch too cool for swimming at the beach (except early October).

When to sail most effectively

Greece's sailing season extends from early April through early to mid-November. While you sail in April, May, or June, you'll usually pay less and get the opportunity to explore the islands when they're particularly lush, green, and in blossom. Since the peak season ended in September, October is less crowded, with rates once again going down, and the water is especially perfect for swimming.

Mountain hiking's ideal season

The green mountain environment is covered in vibrant wildflowers and the weather is frequently perfect for a hike, making April and May excellent months for trekking in the highlands. Another great season is in October when the summer's scorching temperatures start to moderate and the mountains are transformed by the vivid fall colors of the autumn foliage.

Best Time to Save Money

In comparison to the summer, hotels are substantially more affordable throughout the low season (December to March) and shoulder season (April, May, October, and November). There are seldom savings in such areas because the cost of transportation, food, and beverages typically remains the same throughout the year. The best periods to travel are in late May, early June, late September, and early October if you want nice weather and affordable lodgings. There are no assurances, but visitors are frequently pleasantly surprised by the weather during the first three weeks of October.

The best nightlife can be found on Mykonos, Paros, Ios, and Santorini. July and August are the ideal months to go out and party, dance, and listen to live DJs. Late June and early September are also favorable times to visit Mykonos. From late May to early October, Santorini offers lively nightlife.

June to September is ideal if you desire a beach vacation. Anytime between April and early November would be perfect if you're more interested in peace, isolation, sightseeing, and romance.

Greece Travel Seasons

High Season (middle of June to mid-September)

The summer months are considered Greece's prime season, which means that at this time you'll probably encounter oppressive heat, exorbitant pricing, and a throng of tourists that will seem to make up half of Europe. The positives include the best boat and other transit schedules, a hopping nightlife, and the opening of all resorts and attractions.

Shoulder Season (April through Mid-June and Mid-September through October)

Greece is undoubtedly best visited in the shoulder seasons of late spring and early fall. You may typically find some of the best weather of the year during this time, get better hotel deals, and are less likely to run across large crowds of travelers. The majority of locations will be open, and ferry services and flights are still widely accessible.

Low Season (November through March)

Greece has relatively warm winters, so you won't have to worry about subzero temperatures, though there are plenty of chilly, rainy, and gloomy days between November and February and rain is frequent.

Skiing is feasible because there is snow in the mountains. Winter is the best time to travel since there are fewer visitors around, making it less stressful, and because hotel and airfare costs are at their lowest. Be aware that there may be closures of numerous hotels, eateries, and tourist destinations, in addition to reduced ferry and aircraft service.

Key dates for your calendar

Greek Orthodox Easter Holy Week, April-May

The solemn display of Greek Orthodox Easter will move you, regardless of your level of religious observance. The most significant and colorful holiday for Greeks, who throng back to their home villages and islands, is this week-long celebration of candlelit processions, midnight pyrotechnics, Lenten treats, and rotating Easter Sunday lambs on spits. Greece has a variety of Easter customs, from the well-known flying urns of Corfu to the incinerating of Judas' effigy in Monemvasia. But the midnight mass on Good Friday is sure to be a highlight no matter where you are. Greeks are marching to the nearest church to hear somber Easter anthems, so grab a light and join the procession.

Athens and Epidaurus Festival runs from June to September

The famed Athens and Epidaurus Festival reigns supreme during Greece's summer festival season outdoors. The two best-preserved ancient stone arenas in the world—the Theatre of Epidaurus from the fourth century BC, renowned for its crystal-clear acoustics, and the Odeon of Herodes Atticus beneath the Parthenon—serve as the setting for the action. You may see everyone from Helen Mirren to Nana Mouskouri, as well as works by Beckett, Nana Mouskouri, and Nana Mouskouri, during this three-month explosion of music, drama, dance, and visual arts. What is the most buzz? Seeing plays by classical Greek writers like Sophocles or Aristophanes played in the location where they were originally performed

November: Thessaloniki International Film Festival and the Athens Marathon

Thessaloniki's yearly International Film Festival, Greece's Sundance, is a great opportunity to explore the delicious cuisine and hip atmosphere of Athens' historic northern neighbor. You can enjoy this laid-back and hospitable port town at its best during the festival, which is held in early November and sees the entire city throw out the red carpet, with concurrent activities at seaside pubs, dockside cafes, and ancient squares.

The traditional Athens Marathon, the most renowned footrace in the world, begins in November as well. Long-distance runners from all over the world take on the once-in-a-lifetime challenge of retracing the fabled steps of Pheidippides. Seeing the racers cross the finish line in the ancient Olympic stadium leaves a lasting impression. You can count on hearing music, live discussion, and feverish excitement.

Travel Costs to Greece

Category	Cost
Airfare	$4,300
Accommodations	$6,000
Transportation	$1,000
Food	$1,440
Activities	$1,000
Total Greece Trip Budget	$13,740

Average Costs of Travel to Greece

Average Solo Traveler

The average cost for one person to visit Greece for a week is

$896-$2,654

($128-$379 per day)

Food, Travel, and Sightseeing: $32 to $67 per day for one person's daily expenses

Flights: $360 to $1,615 for economy

Lodging: $52 to $69 per night for one 2 or 3-star hotel room or $78 to $95 per night for a 1-bed vacation rental

Average Couple's Trip

The average cost for a couple to visit Greece for a week is

$1,487-$4,737

($212-$677 per day)

Food, Travel, and Sightseeing: $65 to $134 per day for two people's daily expenses

Flights: $720 to $3,229 for economy

Lodging: $52 to $69 per night for one 2 or 3-star hotel room or $78 to $95 per night for a 1-bed vacation rental

Average Family Vacation

The average cost for 4 people to visit Greece for a week is

$2,973-$9,193

($425-$1,313 per day)

Food, Travel, and Sightseeing: $129 to $268 per day for four people's daily expenses

Flights: $1,440 to $6,459 for economy

Lodging: $105 to $137 per night for two 2 or 3-star hotel rooms or $117 to $143 per night for a 2-bed vacation rental

Travel to Greece on a budget

Budget Solo Traveler

The lowest cost for one person to visit Greece for a week is

$688-$2,476

($98-$354 per day)

Food, Travel, and Sightseeing: $16 to $33 per day for one person's daily expenses

Flights: $360 to $1,615 for economy

Lodging: $36 to $42 per night for one 1-star hotel room or $74 to $105 per night for a 1-bed vacation rental

Budget Couple's Trip

The lowest cost for a couple to visit Greece for a week is

$1,167-$4,314

($167-$616 per day)

Food, Travel, and Sightseeing: $33 to $65 per day for two people's daily expenses

Flights: $720 to $3,229 for economy

Lodging: $36 to $42 per night for one 1-star hotel room or $74 to $105 per night for a 1-bed vacation rental

Budget Family Vacation

The lowest cost for 4 people to visit Greece for a week is

$2,327-$8,305

($332-$1,186 per day)

Food, Travel, and Sightseeing: $65 to $130 per day for four people's daily expenses

Flights: $1,440 to $6,459 for economy

Lodging: $72 to $84 per night for two 1-star hotel rooms or $110 to $156 per night for a 2-bed vacation rental

The Price of a Luxurious Greece Vacation

Luxury Solo Traveler

The high-end price for one person to visit Greece for a week is

$1,925-$10,491

($275-$1,499 per day)

Food, Travel, and Sightseeing: $64 to $134 per day for one person's daily expenses

Flights: $907 to $3,997 for first class

Lodging: $95 to $178 per night for one 4 or 5-star hotel room or $464 to $926 per night for a preferred vacation rental

Luxury Couple's Trip

The high-end price for a couple to visit Greece for a week is

$3,287-$15,434

($470-$2,205 per day)

Food, Travel, and Sightseeing: $129 to $269 per day for two people's daily expenses

Flights: $1,814 to $7,995 for first class

Lodging: $95 to $178 per night for one 4 or 5-star hotel room or $464 to $926 per night for a preferred vacation rental

Luxury Family Vacation

The high-end price for 4 people to visit Greece for a week is

$6,568-$28,107

($938-$4,015 per day)

Food, Travel, and Sightseeing: $258 to $537 per day for four people's daily expenses

Flights: $3,628 to $15,990 for first class

Lodging: $189 to $356 per night for two 4 or 5-star hotel rooms or $697 to $1,393 per night for a preferred vacation rental

Getting Around in Greece and the Greek Island

Domestic flights

Olympic Air and Aegean Airlines are the two main domestic airlines in Greece. While Sky Express and Astra Airlines (in Thessaloniki) operate some charter flights throughout the summer, they manage the majority of domestic flights.

In Greece, 42 airports are open to the public, of which 15 are for international travel and 27 are for domestic travel.

Any airport that operates as an international airport will offer direct international flights that will take you directly to that area, avoiding Athens, especially during the high season. So, for instance, if you wanted to skip Athens altogether and go straight to Mykonos or Santorini (Thera), you could.

All domestic airports are open during the peak travel season; however, some don't operate at all other times. This means that you will need to use other modes of transportation, such as ferries, to reach particular islands or specific sites.

As with the majority of airlines, it is best to purchase your tickets as soon as possible because you will have a greater selection, pay less, and have more flexibility in selecting the day and time of your journey. Check all the allowances included with your tickets, including the baggage and carry-on restrictions, as you may incur additional fees or possibly be denied boarding if you don't.

Ferries

In Greece, there are several different ferry options, each with unique benefits and features. Under the management of various private ferry firms, they travel over a vast, adaptable, and intricate network of ferry lines that serve every island and port in Greece.

You can choose from three different types of ferries:

the traditional multiple-deck car-and-passenger ferries. The cheapest tickets are often for deck seats, and they typically include two or three classes plus cabins. Although these boats travel at a slower rate than others, they are the most dependable in bad weather. These are the ones you choose if you get seasick because they wobble the least while at sea.

The hydrofoils are more compact ferries. They are also known as "Flying Dolphins." There is minimal room to walk around and seating that is similar to those on an airliner. Although they are highly quick watercraft, they also have the propensity to be vulnerable to bad weather and are readily grounded. If you are prone to seasickness, they might not be too understanding. They can be found in the ports that link the islands in the same cluster.

76

The quickest and most modern ferries are catamarans. They are sometimes referred to as "Flying Cats" or "Sea Jets." There will typically be lounges and other facilities onboard, and some can carry cars. They frequently also cost the most.

Locally, you can also discover caiques, which are simple, traditional boats made to transport passengers short distances around an island or across to another island. They typically have no restrooms, only outside seating with hard wooden benches, and will swing a lot. Each time, they carry only a small number of passengers. They are great for beautiful and enjoyable sailing, though.

Except for the Ionian Islands, all of the major island groups including Crete may be reached from Athens via the ports of Piraeus and Rafina. Lavrion, which is close to Athens and more effective for some of the islands because it is closer to them, is another option.

The ports of Patra, Igoumenitsa, and Kyllini link the Ionian Islands to the mainland. Some boats allow you to purchase a ticket moments before boarding, even during high season, but it isn't wise to take the chance. The best course of action is to make an advance ticket purchase, preferably online. You may accomplish that by using Ferry Hopper, which offers you the chance to compare and select from all of the available routes and tickets.

It's wise to arrive at the port a few hours before the ferry is scheduled to arrive. If it's a typical car-and-passenger ferry, getting there two hours beforehand might be preferable, especially if you intend to bring your car with you. In this manner, you can get on the plane easily and skip most of the subsequent lines. Keep your ticket and passport somewhere convenient to access them in case the ferry crew or port officials ask to see them.

Trains

A wonderful way to unwind, relax, and take in the stunning landscape is to travel around mainland Greece by rail. Greece has quick, dependable, clean, and well-maintained trains. Take into account that the train travel from Athens to Thessaloniki takes about 4 hours to give an idea of the times.

The Greek railway company, Trainose, is in charge of running the trains in Greece. Both city trains and trains linking Greek cities are available. The Intercity Network is the quickest of those. It links Athens to the Peloponnese, Chalkida, Volos City, Central Greece, and Northern Greece (Kiato, Corinth, and Patras).

The train from Diakofto to Kalavryta, the Pelion steam train, and the train from Katakolo to Ancient Olympia are among the "tourism lines" that the Intercity Network also runs. These routes are more thematic, focused on sightseeing, and have specific cultural value for the Greeks. Every stop along all three itineraries is noteworthy from a cultural perspective. If you're interested in using them, check the timetables and make reservations in advance. These lines are often open throughout the summer and on holidays.

Economy class and first-class seats are available on intercity trains. With a folding table, the first-class seats offer extra privacy. You have more storage space and legroom as a result of them. There is less privacy in economy class seats, yet they are still relatively wide at the shoulders and pleasant.

Even though you can purchase tickets at the station, it is not suggested to do so during the busiest times. Through the Trainose website or mobile app, you can purchase tickets online.

The KTEL buses

The bus system that links each city in Greece with the others is made up primarily of KTEL buses. To get through Greece, they are a quick and reasonably priced method. The intra-regional and local bus kinds are under the KTEL umbrella.

The buses that link cities within a region are known as intra-regional ones, and they use major thoroughfares to accomplish so. The neighborhood roads, which connect the several towns of an area with one another, will be used by the local ones rather than the interstate. On the island and in regions where there are concentrations of communities to explore, you can locate local KTEL buses.

The two main KTEL stations in Athens, Liosion station and Kifissos station, are where the majority of inter-regional buses depart from. Buses heading north from Athens to Thessaloniki stop at Liosion Station, and buses heading south from Athens to the Peloponnese stop at Kifissos Station.

The following are a few of the most well-known Ktel buses in Greece:

- Ktel Attikis (you can use it to go to Sounio)

- Ktel Thessaloniki (if you want to go to Thessaloniki by bus)
- Ktel Volos (if you want to visit Pelion or take the boat to the Sporades islands)
- Ktel Argolidas (if you want to visit Nafplio, Mycenae, and Epidaurus
- Ktel Fokidas (if you want to visit the archaeological site of Delphi)
- Ktel Ioanninon (if you want to visit Ioannina and Zagorohoria)
- Ktel Mykonos (public transport around the island)
- Ktel Santorini (public transport around the island)
- Ktel Milos (public transport around the island)
- Ktel Naxos (public transport around the island)
- Ktel Paros (public transport around the island)
- Ktel Kefalonia (public transport around the island)
- Ktel Corfu (public transport around the island)
- Ktel Rhodes (public transport around the island)
- Ktel Chania (Crete) (public transport around the Chania area)

Taxis

In Athens and around Greece, finding a taxi is simple. There are taxi ranks outside of ports, airports, train stations, and the busiest areas of Athens and the Greek islands.

All you need to do to stop a cab is move to the side of the road and raise your hand. If you compare it to other European nations, it is relatively affordable and a useful method of transportation for short distances.

Cars and Car rentals

When you are in a given location and need to move around, a car is the best and most secure mode of transportation.

In Greece and the Greek islands, there are automobile rental companies in the most well-known locations. Greece's major road systems are up to date and in good condition, but the country's smaller, meandering rural roads require repair.

Useful Greek Phrases for Travelers

- Yeia sou! "Yah-soo": Hello
- Kalimera "Kah-lee-meh-rah": Good Morning
- Kalispera "Kah-lee-speh-rah": Good Evening
- Kalinikta "Kah-lee-nee-khtah": Good Night
- Andio "Ahn-dee-oh": Goodbye
- Efharisto "Ehf-khah-ree-stoh": Thank you
- Parakalo "Pah-rah-kah-loh": Please and You're Welcome
- Signomi "See-gnoh-mee": Excuse me and/or Sorry
- Opa! "Oh-pa": Oops!
- Yamas "Yah-mahs": To Our Health (used like "cheers")
- Fili mou "Fee-lee moo": My Friend
- Kefi "keh-fee": Fun or Joy
- Siga Siga "see-gah, see-gah": Slowly, Slowly
- Nai "Neh": Yes
- Oxi "Oh-khee": No
- Endaxi "ehn-dah-ksee": It's OK
- Ela "eh-la": Come or Come On
- Me lene "Meh-leh-neh": My name is

Greece Packing List

- Compact Portable Charger
- Storage cubes
- Private Internet Access (PIA)
- Water Shoes with Mesh Straps
- Greece Power Adapter
- Filter-equipped water bottle
- Fast-Drying Travel Towel
- Cheap Underwater Camera
- Towel Set for Cooling
- Swimsuit Coverup
- Avoid Pickpockets by Wearing a Neck Wallet
- Greece travel insurance
- Luggage Locks That Have Been Approved by the TSA
- female urination apparatus
- comfortable Flats
- Bracelets that repel mosquitoes
- Scarf/Shawl
- (Food Poisoning Fix) Activated Charcoal

CHAPTER THREE
Where to Stay in Greece

The 8 Best Areas to Stay in Greece

Athens —Best Place to Stay in Greece

Athens is every traveler's ideal city. Athens is positively dripping with historical treasures, and it's impossible not to be impressed. The Acropolis is only one aspect of it. You'll have so much to see, from the Temple of Zeus to the Roman Agora and Hadrian's Library, that you'll want to make sure you have enough time to see it all. A once-in-a-lifetime experience, marveling at these ancient temples and monuments' ruins.

Athens is not only brimming with historical treasures, but it also has a thriving trendy scene right now.

Top Recommended Hotels in Athens

- 5-star: Grande Bretagne
- 4-star: Electra Palace
- 3-star: Phaedra
- Boutique Hotel: AthensWas
- New Hotel: xenodocheio Milos
- For Families: Ava
- For Couples: Gatsby
- Hotel Pool: Four Seasons
- Acropolis View: Electra Palace
- Airport Hotel: Sofitel
- Ferry Port: Triton Hotel
- Beach Resort: Four Season

Best Airbnb in Athens – Urban Studios Acropolis View

It's a little studio apartment that only has room for two people to fit comfortably. On the other hand, the private balcony provides a HUGE view of the Acropolis. In the center of Monastiraki, a well-known and popular tourist destination is this stylish tiny studio apartment. A mini-fridge, a tea kettle, and a private toilet are provided despite the absence of a kitchen.

Best Hostel in Athens – Mosaikon

Mosaikon is a mid-range hostel that won't let you down, even though it isn't the cheapest of the inexpensive hostels available. In addition to its outstanding location, Mosaikon is renowned for its immaculate dorm rooms. Syntagma Square, which is bustling with upscale bars and restaurants, is only 800 meters away from them. The Mosaikon Hostel's other best feature? The Acropolis is seen from the rooftop terrace of this building.

Best Hotel in Athens – Athens Lights

In the heart of Athens, there is a place called Athens Lights. Athens Lights is a popular lodging option in Greece because it has all the bells and whistles and is reasonably priced. Together with the immaculately clean rooms, it is private. A pleasant touch is the balconies, which are furnished with outdoor furniture for relaxing in the sun.

Ioannina – Best Place to Stay in Greece for Families

At the geographic heart of Greece, Ioannina encircles the picturesque Lake Pamvotida. Even the monastery of Saint Nicholas Philanthropinon, which is located in the middle of a little island in the lake, is there. Both Athens and Thessaloniki may be reached in just three to four hours by car. As a result, it is easily reachable by both public transit and renting a car.

Ioannina is the perfect place in Greece to travel with your family because of the quiet surroundings and the peace of Lake Pamvotida's still waters. The youngsters will enjoy relaxing in the Ioannina Castle, which was constructed in 528 AD. It is truly magical. There are several kid-friendly restaurants and museums in the historic part of the city, which is only accessible by foot.

A charming little lakeside village called Ioannina. Given its size, you can guarantee your bottom dollar that Ioannina has some charming lodging options. You and your family will find your little piece of home in Ioannina, from charming studio apartments to exquisitely designed hotels.

Best Airbnb in Ioannina – Paris's Central Studio

You and your family will love this Ioannina Airbnb. This studio in the heart of Ioannina has two beds and one bathroom, and it sleeps four people without any problems. The area is near to everything you need and is bright and cozy. It is exquisitely decorated and incredibly contemporary. If you're traveling with a young child, you can also choose to add a baby cot.

Best Hostel in Ioannina – Backpackers and Travelers

In June 2019, this hostel for backpackers on a budget first opened its doors. Since the beginning, Ioannina has only had one hostel. Due to the limited quantity of six-bed dorm rooms, this hostel may be the ideal choice for you depending on the number and age of your children. With basic dorm rooms, this hostel has a very cozy and pleasant atmosphere.

Best Hotel in Ioannina – Kentrikon

The stunningly designed Kentrikon is situated in the center of Ioannina. containing closed windows and walls made of natural stone. A little bit of the modern world has a feeling of colliding with the Middle Ages. An additional significant benefit is the full American breakfast buffet.

Santorini is probably what comes to mind when you think of the Greek islands. It's impossible not to fall in love with the charming white and blue homes that line the slopes. Drool-worthy, they are. Booking the next flight to Santorini is a good idea for couples who need a serious dose of passion in their relationship.

This enchanted island is also home to meandering roads, ancient ruins, crimson beaches, and black-sand beaches in addition to its architectural Instagram-worthy splendor. Take a boat out to the Santorini Caldera if you're feeling daring, and explore a volcano crater while you're there.

Best Airbnb in Santorini – Santorini Seclusion

This Airbnb is quite the find, and it's conveniently close to Fira's center. If you want to explore more of the island, the major bus stop is close by. Visitors will feel right at home in this private room, which is full of thoughtful details and has a cute balcony. Couples, book your trip to Santorini today for an amazing experience.

Best Hostel in Santorini – Fira Backpackers Place

The downtown Fira region is where Fira Backpackers Place is situated. You're sure to be pleased with your choice of lodging at this hostel, whether you and your significant other decide to save money by staying in the dorm rooms or getting a private room. Social rooms and a living room with a large TV and a selection of DVDs to choose from are also available.

Best Hotel in Santorini – Cyclades Hotel

Fira may be reached on foot from the Cyclades Hotel, which is also close to a bus station. Along with this, a supermarket and bakery are also close by. You can easily see the entire island of Santorini from there because it is in the ideal location. Santorini hotels are also very hard to find at a better price.

Thessaloniki is Greece's second-largest city after Athens. For travelers on a tight budget, it's also among the finest locations to stay in Greece. Importantly, Thessaloniki is quite simple to reach and navigate in and out of; there is a sizable international airport, as well as numerous buses and trains. You also won't need to bother about buying ferry tickets to bounce from island to island. To and from Istanbul, you can even board a night bus.

Thessaloniki was established in 315 BC and offers several breathtaking sites to see, including the White Tower, the Arch of Galerius, and Aristotelous Square. As a port city, there are no beaches, but there are a lot of tranquil waterfront eateries to enjoy and a lengthy stretch of pavement to follow along the shoreline.

A visit to Thessaloniki, also referred to as Greece's cultural capital is a must for anybody visiting the country. There are many events to take part in, including film and art festivals.

Best Airbnb in Thessaloniki – Cozy Apartment in the Heart of Thessaloniki

This is a fantastic deal if you're four friends seeking a contemporary apartment in Thessaloniki's city center. One bedroom and a comfortable sofa bed are both present in this one-bedroom apartment. Along with many markets, restaurants, and cafes, it is handy for all forms of public transit. When you rent this Airbnb, you won't have to worry about needing a taxi. Additionally, a kitchen is available for you to use so you may cook your meals and save money.

Best Hostel in Thessaloniki – Crossroads

Crossroads is located close to the Byzantine Walls and ten minutes from the city's core. There are three distinct dorm rooms, and the dorm beds are inexpensive. You're guaranteed to meet someone at Crossroads because of its friendly vibe.

Best Hotel in Thessaloniki – Pella

Pella Hotel is the place for you if you don't want to overpay for a dorm room. The cost of this conveniently situated hotel is reasonable, and it gives visitors quick access to all that Thessaloniki has to offer, from the local markets to the Byzantine fortress.

Mykonos – Coolest Place to Stay in Greece

The second-most populated island in Greece is without any doubt Mykonos. It's renowned for having an incredible party scene that even attracts celebrities on their luxurious yachts.

Mykonos is a fun-loving, stylish island that can party. I've served my time in Mykonos, so you can trust me. Of course, Mykonos is more than simply a party island. There are well-known windmills, the remains of Delos, an archaeological museum, and a ton of breathtaking and recognizable white and blue structures.

Best Airbnb in Mykonos – Studio with Garden View

This Mykonos beach house Airbnb is in the ideal location for visiting the beach, Chora, as well as the local bus. The main town will be a short stroll away. Everything you need for a comfortable stay is in a straightforward, spotless room.

Best Hostel in Mykonos – MyCocoon Hostel

The MyCocoon Hostel is located in Kaminaki, directly across from the pedestrian entry to Mykonos Town. MyCocoon is the hostel to pick for a stay in Mykonos with a price tag like this and the wonderfully designed furniture and stylings of this hostel. It's among the best places to stay in Greece.

Best Hotel in Mykonos – Ilio Maris

One of Greece's finest hotels is Ilio Maris. Ilio Maris is a luxurious resort with stunning views of the sea and well-known windmills. If you want to indulge a little, this is the place to do it even though the prices are double or treble what you'd pay at a hostel. This stunning hotel, which is in Mykonos Town's heart, will take your breath away.

Meteora – One of the Most Unique Places to Stay in Greece

Meteora is a must-see city, even though its name may not be particularly familiar. One of Greece's real treasures, it. Eastern Orthodox monasteries are housed among the distinctive rock formations of Meteora, which are famous for their cliff-side locations and unusual rock formations. The most unusual sights to see and places to visit in all of Greece are these clifftop monasteries.

Most significant cities may be reached by train from Meteora, which is situated in central Greece. It is possible to visit Meteora in a single day from Athens, but you'll have the most fun if you spend at least one night there to take in the scenery without feeling rushed — or in a fog from waking up at five in the morning to catch a train.

Best Airbnb in Meteora – Escape to Meteora

Escape to this lovely Meteora Airbnb in Kalambaka that is encircled by the granite formations of Meteora. Your exclusive use of the apartment is guaranteed with this rental. The classic design is combined with contemporary comforts in a lovely way.

Best Hostel in Meteora – Meteora Central Hostel

In the center of Kalambaka, the Meteora Central Hostel is situated. Although the house was constructed in 1950, it was only recently opened. The lovely wood floors are as lovely as the brick and stone walls. Everything is brand new and of a high standard, including the furniture and decor. Outside, in the little, green backyard, there is also a space that is ideal for practicing some yoga in the morning or just relaxing with a cup of tea.

Best Hotel in Meteora – Mythos Guesthouse

If you want to stay in Meteora but are on a budget and still want a convenient, peaceful, lovely location, the Mythos Guesthouse is a great option. Worth the money, A charming tiny balcony that provides a wonderful side view of the rock formations is located outside each room.

Crete – Where to Stay in Greece for Adventure

The lovely Greek island of Crete is one of the best places to stay in Greece for adventure. It is the biggest Greek city and has a lot to offer. If you're in Greece and crave a serious dose of adventure, head over to Crete.

The three major cities on the island—Heraklion, Chania, and Rethymno—are where visitors typically choose to stay. Heraklion is the largest and busiest of the three. Chania is smaller and more picturesque. Rethymno is the most exquisite of the three. Rethymno is a very beautiful city that is situated in the middle of Chania and Heraklion, the two main cities. You'll therefore be ideally situated in the middle of everything.

Best Airbnb in Crete – Luxurious Family Apartment

This family apartment offers breathtaking views of Rethymno's Old Town and its castle. It is a three-bedroom, two-bathroom apartment that can accommodate seven people in total. Therefore, this is undoubtedly the perfect location for you and your other adrenaline-addict buddies if you're traveling in a group. You'll adore the private terrace with its furnishings made of wood and plants. Additionally, there is a sizable kitchen where you and your friends can prepare meals for the family.

Best Hostel in Crete – Rethymno Youth Hostel

When seeking a place to stay in Crete, Rethymno Youth Hostel is unrivaled. A terrace for playing cards, a tiled courtyard ideal for sunbathing, and several options for interaction with others abound. You're guaranteed to like staying in this area, which is located in the center of Old Town.

Best Hotel in Crete – Hotel Ideon

Greece's island hotels, especially those on the island of Crete, are renowned for being a little on the extravagant side of things. However, you may receive the most comfort at Hotel Ideon for a reasonable price. You may enjoy a fantastic breakfast buffet while staying in the heart of Rethymno at Hotel Ideon.

Naxos – Where to Stay in Greece for Greek Island Life

The island of Naxos is rugged, verdant, and home to stunning ancient ruins. Even a hilltop fortress from the thirteenth century can be visited. However, Naxos transforms into quite a party scene during the summer peak season because of the abundance of pubs, nightclubs, and bouzoukis. From jazz to Greek music to hip-hop, you can hear all different types of music.

The most gorgeous beach in Naxos is Agios Prokopios Beach, which is only 6 kilometers from Naxos town. It is renowned for its stunning golden sands and clear blue waters. A beverage can be enjoyed under one of the many sunbeds and umbrellas that are available.

Given its proximity to the main town and the fact that it is only 2 km away, Agios Georgios Beach is particularly popular for windsurfing and people in general. Naturally, Asia Anna Beach with its lovely fishing harbor offers the ideal snorkeling waters.

Best Airbnb in Naxos – Nikiforos Apartment

For those travelers who desire some peace as well as private beach access, this private studio apartment with one bedroom and one bathroom is ideal. A 10-minute stroll will take you to Chora Beach and the castle from St. George Beach. Additionally, the neighborhood has a grocery store, coffee shop, bakery, and restaurant.

Best Hotel in Naxos – Sweet Home Naxos

Sweet Home Naxos is a stunning, family-run hotel with a charming design that is only a short stroll from St. George Beach. While maintaining a slight Greek flair, it is contemporary, clear, and clean. You'll like relaxing on the terrace and having quick access to the sandy beach from here.

The best Greek island hotels and where to stay for private beaches and caldera views

Corfu

The gorgeous, green island where Odysseus was shipwrecked is a wonderful mash-up of several cultural influences, including those of the British who ruled the island from 1814 to 1864. There are Italianate mansions, ornate palaces, Byzantine, and Venetian architecture. The Ionian Island where the Durrells formerly resided is also renowned for its stunning beaches, the most well-known of which is Sidari, which features wide expanses of fine sand bordered by sandstone bluffs. For less crowded sunbathing, consider taking a day excursion to Corfu's uninhabited Diapontia islands.

Where to stay

Delfino Blu Boutique Hotel

On the northern border of gios Stéfanos Avliotón, the Delfino Blue Boutique has a view across the straits toward the Mathráki and Othon islets and the setting sun. This chic boutique hotel is especially popular with solo travelers, newlyweds, and wedding parties thanks to its exquisite restaurant, impeccable service, and cozy accommodations.

The Merchant's House

The Merchant's House is situated in what is likely Corfu's most tranquil area, halfway up the north face of Mt. Pandokrátor. When there is no moon, the stars are magnificent, and when the surrounding tavernas close, owls and crickets provide a spooky nocturnal soundtrack. The restoration of this 17th-century building from the Venetian era as a boutique bed and breakfast was largely based on meticulous attention to detail and hand-crafted components.

Domes Miramare Corfu

Dominica Houses The pinnacle of the Ionian Isle is Corfu. Southeast of Corfu Town, in the tranquil community of Moraitika, is this magnificent five-star, adults-only refuge. The essence of the past owners, the Onassis family, is evident and charming yet unassuming. White, grey, and teal color schemes are used in the interior design to reimagine 1960s style with a modern flair. A 400-meter-long beach is fronted by ancient olive trees that stand proudly among palm trees and gardens.

Crete

Greece's largest island, which stretches from the Venetian harbor of Chania in the west to Sitia's mostly deserted beaches in the east, is a concentrated sample of what the nation does well. It has a variety of landscapes, mouthwatering cuisine, and breathtaking seascapes. There is much to excite cultural enthusiasts, from touring the Minoan palace of Knossos to taking a boat from Elounda to Spinalonga, the leper island featured in Victoria Hislop's best-selling novel. Hike Samaria, the longest gorge in Europe, to immerse yourself in nature.

Nana Princess

The stunning "space age" spa of Nana Princess is arguably the most opulent in all of Crete. There are modern Nuvola treatment beds, aromatherapy showers, stunning treatment rooms, and relaxation areas, as well as a solarium, in addition to the typical steam room, saunas, and pools. There are two swimming pools close to the seashore, a play pool in the kids' club, and a secluded, coarse-sand beach with plenty of sun loungers.

White River Cottages

Once upon a time, during the olive-picking season, the people of Péfki village lived seasonally in this hamlet of stone-built, flat-roofed homes. The cottages, which are now self-catering lodging, are all clean-lined and rustic; picture whitewashed stone and polished cypress-wood trunks. Natural rock outcrops that were left in place to be incorporated into a cottage's floor layout give it a style that is virtually troglodytic.

Porto Veneziano

This immaculately stylish three-star hotel, which fronts Chania's magnificent Venetian harbor, is close to the region's top attractions and a 15-minute stroll from a sandy beach. With several creative additions, including a machine to polish shoes, the interior design skillfully combines modern and cozy elements. The breakfast is excellent here, and it's served in a cute little eating area with a stunning view of the harbor.

Abaton Island Resort & Spa

A slope leads down to the sea at this modern, luxurious resort in the Cycladic style. Low-white buildings reflect pools and water features that resemble lagoons, and enormous glass walls provide unending views of the ocean. A large infinity pool with daybeds and wet beds, a kiddie pool, and a heated indoor spa pool are just a few of the features. There is a sauna, gym, beauty salon, and steam room inside the Elemis spa. On the sandy stretch of beach, there are many sun loungers.

Stella Island Luxury Resort & Spa

A tropical "Love Island" ambiance, excellent service, and an adults-only aquatic wonderland define this destination. The chic resort is constructed around one of Europe's largest lagoon pools and is entirely white with plenty of blonde wood, canvas, and bamboo (inflatable giant flamingos are a nice extra touch). Additionally, visitors can make advantage of the organized beach and other amenities of Stella Village, a neighboring sister resort.

Monastery Estate Venetian Harbor

A monastery both in name and in essence. Stone arches, tall stone walls, and a sizable portion of the city's original Roman fortifications—which can be viewed through glass floors on various levels—are striking original elements. In addition to the tight (but evocative) original stone-built Turkish hammam, there is a small jetted pool and a relaxation room. The hotel's Mon.Es restaurant serves creative and ample Cretan cuisine.

Avra Imperial Hotel

This opulent resort is located near a section of Kolymvari's shingle beach, just outside of Chania. The resort's major attraction is a sizable pool with a glass wall, which is flanked by rooms on three stories and several restaurants that are surrounded by little lawns, water features, and banks of meticulously maintained plants. Simple, durable furniture with calming colors are used (beige, charcoal, cream).

Kapsaliana Village Hotel

This exquisitely restored collection of stone village homes, which formerly belonged to the Arkadi monastery, is a throwback to rural Crete with plenty of contemporary flourishes. It is centered around a sizable pool and is surrounded by lush grounds. A restaurant that serves organic food is also present.

Rhodes

The Knights Templar-built fortress walls and the winding cobblestone streets lined with medieval inns in Rhodes' Unesco-designated old town make it truly unique (it was once one of the Seven Wonders of the Ancient World). In addition to a string of sandy beaches where tavernas serve pitaroudia, a chickpea, tomato, and onion fritter, and other regional specialties, you can find narrow winding roads further afield that lead to lush valleys and tiny mountain villages, including dazzling white Lindos, topped by its 4th-century acropolis.

Atrium Prestige, Rhodes

This enormous spa complex is nestled into a green hillside on Rhodes' quieter south coast and has everything you need for a stress-free Greek vacation: breathtaking sea views, a wide variety of eating options, and an excellent spa. Atrium Prestige's rooms are spacious and cozy, with a traditional aesthetic. Private pools are included in the top-tier suites.

Koukos Traditional Guesthouse

This quirky, retro-styled guesthouse in Rhodes' new town hits the spot with its liberally strewn antiques and whimsical, cuckoo-themed decor if you're looking for a big dose of Greek fun. It's located above a bustling Greek taverna. It almost resembles a rustic Alpine chalet with its stone façade, wooden balconies, and cuckoo clocks, but when you enter, Greek pop music is playing loudly on the speakers. The hotel manages to successfully tread the fine line between vintage and corny.

Kókkini Porta Rossa

The chic boutique hotel Kókkini Porta Rossa can be found in Rhodes' old town on a quiet residential street. It provides a luxurious setting, impeccable decor, fine dining, and personalized service from the Greek owners. Greek antiques and Rhodian artifacts from their collection, which they have carefully chosen, add to the property's genuine charm.

Marco Polo Mansion

The hotel in Old Town is arguably the most atmospheric. This former Ottoman official's home has a bohemian flair, lots of laughter, and a welcoming atmosphere that makes it feel more like a favorite uncle's house than a chic bed and breakfast. The decor in Marco Polo's home looks like it came straight out of a Taschen book. It combines dark wood furniture, Turkish carpets, Indian wall hangings, and Bavarian rugs, all of which are brilliantly illuminated by lime-washed walls in vibrant colors.

Santorini

- 5-Star: Grace
- 4-Star: Tsitouras Collection
- Boutique: Aenaon Villas
- Midrange: Enigma
- Cheap: Kavalari
- Family Hotel: Aria Suites
- Beach Resort: Istoria
- Best New Hotel: Sea Breeze
- Best Pool: Nous
- Best Caldera Sunset View: Astra Suites

Kapari Natural Resort, Santorini

The laid-back Cyclades style of life is exemplified by Kapari Natural Resort, which is perched on a Santorini hillside. All visitors to the family-run hotel are treated to peaceful whitewashed rooms with spectacular views, an infinity pool, and a restaurant serving the best Greek food.

Canaves Oia, Santorini

The Canaves Oia Hotel, which is laid-back, stylish, and modern, is the ideal place to stay for couples looking for a romantic getaway. Santorini's bleached-white aesthetic is reflected in the rooms, which were modified from the original caverns. Bespoke Italian decorations serve as a reminder of the elegance you will experience. The infinity pool with a swim-up bar and Aegean views at the hotel is the place to be at sunset.

Grace Hotel, Santorini

The Grace Hotel is a seductive Mediterranean haven where you may unwind. With champagne upon arrival, personnel who are constantly checking in, and an unmatched backdrop, this clifftop resort positioned over the renowned Caldera coastline ensures that your stay will be memorable.

Perivolas Hotel, Santorini

The captivating Perivolas Hotel in Santorini marries breathtaking views with a rich history. The hand-dug rooms and suites have built-in beds made of concrete and traditional Santorinian architecture and design. The hotel is close enough to the top eateries, stores, attractions, and villages that it won't be overrun by tourists.

Bellonias Villas, Santorini

The seasonal Bellonias Villas is open from April to mid-October and are located above the Kamari black-sand beach and amid the ancient Thira hilly landscape. The hotel's outside is smooth stucco with clean lines and arched archways, similar to the old structures on the island, while its contemporary and understated. Elia, the hotel's namesake restaurant, is a great choice for dinner if you want sweeping sea views.

Vedema, Santorini

The Vedema Resort in Santorini is as welcoming as it is gorgeous, situated in a great area constructed around 400-year-old wine cellars. Each of the 45 apartments, which have stunning views of the sea or vineyards, is arranged in a village-like structure. The Alati restaurant, housed in a mysterious cave, offers excellent regional cuisine in addition to a fantastic selection of Santorini wines.

On The Rocks, Santorini

The small, intimate On the Rocks, a member of Small Luxury Hotels, is located just 10 minutes from Fira town, the island's capital, and is perched 200 meters above the Santorini Caldera basin. On The Rocks is a top-rated romantic location in Caldera and is ideal for honeymooners. The Cave spa, which features a whirlpool tub and a massage area, offers treatments.

Mykonos

Mykonos, the Cinderella of the Cyclades, was once one of Greece's poorest islands before being "discovered" in the 1960s by shipping magnate Aristotle Onassis and his wife, the former First Lady Jackie Kennedy. LiLo may have given up on her beach club, but Greece's LGBTQ-friendly version of Ibiza continues to draw a modern jet set come here to spend £200 per cocktail at Nammos, work on their tans on the golden sands of Psarou, or take selfies while exploring the sea captain's neighborhood of Little Venice.

Favorite Places to Stay in Mykonos

- 5-star: Mykonos Blu
- 4-star: Panormos Village
- 3-star: Matina
- Mykonos Town: Belvedere
- Ornos: Santa Marina
- Platis Gialos: Branco
- Near Ferry Port: Mykonos Riviera
- Family Hotel: Santa Marina
- New Hotel: Panoptis Escape

The Wild Hotel by Interni, Mykonos

The tranquil Wild Hotel is located on a little beach in a part of the island that has managed to avoid being overrun by tourists. For many years, the neighborhood's village, which was home to Mykonos's most daring fishermen, was known as "the wild one." It is now a primitive, calm refuge that is furnished with every convenience of the contemporary era. With a calming color scheme, the hotel's design combines the old and new aspects of Mykonos to create a homey feeling in each room.

Myconian Villa Collection

This hotel's airy, white-washed rooms, suites, and villas have a lot of amenities like private hot tubs or infinity pools. With five-star hotel service, each one has a truly private and exclusive feel. With secluded terraces and rooms, a stunning infinity pool, and a free shuttle to the neighborhood's private beach, you probably won't feel the need to leave.

Bill & Coo Suites and Lounge, Mykonos

The chic Bill & Coo Suites and Lounge, located in the center of Mykonos, feels a world apart from the bustling party scene on the island and instead provides visitors with a haven where they can unwind in total beachside bliss. The hotel's 32 rooms each have breathtaking views of the setting sun, and it also features two large treatment suites in its spa and outstanding fine dining selections.

Grace Mykonos

The Grace Mykonos is well-known for its accommodations, attentive service, and delectable cuisine (think expertly rendered seafood, creative desserts, and a strong wine list). Subtle luxury and extremely clean lines are the main design features inside. The only bright accents are the artwork in the lobby, which primarily uses a neutral color scheme. Aside from the well-equipped gym and small spa, the pool is the hotel's main attraction.

Belvedere Hotel

The Belvedere offers a private setting and breathtaking panoramas of Chora. Exceptional service and five-star amenities, such as an outdoor sushi bar, a Six Senses spa, and a sapphire-colored pool, make for a luxurious and unwinding stay. A small Greek village-like atmosphere is evoked by the rooms and suites that are dispersed throughout seven buildings in a maze-like layout. The decor is consistent with the rest of the hotel and features marble bathrooms, warm wooden furniture, and immaculate white walls.

Santa Marina, a Luxury Collection Resort

Santa Marina, which offers views of the area's sea, is constructed like a private village in a remote location on a hillside in the southernmost part of the lovely Ornos Bay. Exterior features like stacked stonework and whitewashed walls are in keeping with the straightforward cubist architecture that is unique to the Cyclades. A helipad and a private pier are among the high-end services offered. Water freely flows beneath raised floor tiles to create a zen-like entrance at the Ginkgo Spa.

Hydra

On this charming island, where motorized vehicles are prohibited, peace reigns supreme and is accessible via ferry from Piraeus port in an hour. Lawrence Durrell to Patrick Leigh-Fermorwase was among the many creative types who frequented Hydra over the years, but it was Leonard Cohen, who lived there from 1960 to 1967, who cemented Hydra's reputation. Today's Porto Fino of Greece is home to other top-tier art galleries as well as the magnificent DESTE Foundation, which is housed in the ominous stone structure that formerly served as the island's slaughterhouse.

Hotel Miranda

Hydra, Saronic Islands, Greece

Hotel Miranda, housed in a former sea captain's mansion that has been designated a National Heritage Monument, is a gem of the Hydriot. It was constructed for a Captain Danavasis in the early 19th century, and a hotel has been running there since 1961. A visit here is like going back in time in the best way imaginable. Old wooden sea chests and glass cabinets filled with artifacts from the maritime past are dotted around the hotel. The walls are covered with nautical engravings and black-and-white photos.

Cotommatae Hydra 1810

Hydra, Saronic Islands, Greece

This exquisite boutique hotel was initially constructed in 1810 and has remained in the same family ever since. It was later purchased and modified by a local sponge magnate in 1901. The splendor inside is hidden by high perimeter walls. There are seven rooms altogether, but we particularly like "Pigeons," which was formerly used to house doves.

It has a coffee table made from a piece of an old cart, a private patio with a hydro-massage/whirlpool tub set in planked decking, and is very well-liked by honeymooners.

Syros

Syros, the capital of the Cyclades, is one of the most fascinating cultural gems in the area, dominated by its twin hilltop settlements topped by two churches (one Catholic, one Orthodox). The wealthy local sea captains, who in the 19th century made Syros richer than Piraeus, erected several opulent mansions along the waterfront and had an opera house built on the island's marble-paved central square that was modeled after Milan's La Scala. Atherinopita fish pie and smoke-cured pork louza are two delectable foods to try when visiting Syros.

The Good Life

Poseidonia, Syros, Greece

These stone-built villas are set in an olive grove with a view of one of Syros' most picturesque bays and feature a laid-back atmosphere, plenty of comfort, and eco-friendly amenities. Despite its rural setting,

Poseidonia's tavern-lined resort and sandy beaches are not far away. Due to the island's extreme wilderness, visitors can expect to find numerous olive groves, narrow hiking trails, pristine bays, and nearly deserted beaches here.

5 Hermoupolis Concept Sites

Hermoupolis, Syros, Greece

This hotel is for adults only and is known for its boutique style. It is located next to the famed Apollon Theater in Hermoupolis and is only a short distance from the breathtakingly beautiful Vaporia waterfront. Five of the rooms are doubles. The four superior and deluxe rooms are among the most comfortable (and undoubtedly larger than most) in Syros, where modern hotels are scarce. The standard double is cramped.

Sifnos

Cyclades sizzler Since Nicholas Tselementes, a local author who was born on Sifnos, published the first Greek cookbook there in 1926, the island has been a haven for foodies.

Work up an appetite by visiting the island's tsikaladia pottery workshops (people have been making distinctive brown and white skepastaria earthenware here since 3000 BC) or going on a hike to the enigmatic Venetian citadel of kastro, then settle into a blue cane chair in a neighborhood taverna to enjoy red wine-marinated mastello lamb and other delectables.

Verina Astra

Sifnos, Greece

Amazing views of the infinity pool blending into the azure horizon can be found in this serene, seven-suite retreat. Its stand-alone cottages with sea-viewer races are elegantly understated and have a seductive, secluded cliff-top setting that is instantly calming. The property is surrounded by fragrant gardens.

Kamarotí Suites Hotel

Poulati, Sifnos, Greece

With its boxy Cycladic suites arranged amphitheatrically around a pale green pool and surrounded by Mediterranean gardens and ancient olive trees, Kamarot combines a contemporary vibe with a true sense of place. The location immediately exudes calmness: a quiet valley with tranquil views of the surrounding hills and the sea, with the white smudge of Kastro village winking in the distance. The largest and most picturesque village on the island, Artemonas, is accessible by foot. Apollonia, the bustling island's "capital," is connected to Artemonas by a maze of whitewashed lanes.

Verina Suites

This kid-friendly retreat is tucked away from a sandy bay and is a Cycladic classic with cool white interiors, airy verandas shaded by vibrant bougainvillea, and an olive tree-lined pool. You'll feel right at home thanks to the friendly, welcoming staff. Though you can't see the sea, it's only a short hop across the street to the water. The island's busiest (yet still laid-back) beach, Platis Gialos, offers a wide variety of water sports, beach bars, and taverns. The excellent "fish bar" Omega 3 and the tasty farm-to-table taverna Water and Salt are both just a few sandy steps away.

Naxos

The Cyclades' largest island, Naxos, is frequently overlooked in favor of its glitzy sisters Santorini and Mykonos, but it has plenty to offer, from the golden sands of the popular resort Agios Prokopios to the dune-studded Mikri Vigla's breeze-buffeted bay. Go to mountain villages like Apeiranthos, where the streets are lined with old-fashioned tavernas and marble-clad, or Halki, where the island's famed citrus liqueur Kitro has been produced since 1896 when the sun sets scarlet over those dusky sands.

Favorite Places to Stay in Naxos

- 5-Star: Nissaki
- 4-Star: Iria Beach Art
- 3-Star: Kavos
- Boutique: ELaiolithos
- Cheap: Saint Vlassis
- For Families: Nissaki
- For Couples: ELaiolithos
- Naxos Town: Grotta • Anixis
- Beach Resort: Medusa

Kavos Hotel Naxos

A resort with an ocean view and stone-clad cottages, the Kavos Hotel Naxos is just above the Gios Prokopios resort. It also serves excellent food. The Kavos was among the first constructions here, constructed in 1990 but updated regularly since then, snatching up a prime location just 10 minutes from the closest beach.

Naxian Collection

The very definition of casual luxury. A welcoming and elegant hotel with a chic but understated restaurant is housed in this tranquil hilltop community of stylish, modern villas. Beautiful views of a lagoon and Naxos Town provide an excellent sense of location, and the beach is nearby. You will feel right at home here thanks to the impeccable service and sculptures made from the island's marble.

Ammothines Cycladic Suites

Ammothines is described as having a coastline in the French Atlantic style, with a silky beach, turquoise water, and a group of cozy suites covered in marble. There is a lovely L-shaped swimming pool at the hotel, and the family-run restaurant serves food with Turkish influences.

Skiathos

The northern Sporades Island of Skiathos, which served as the lush and lovely setting for the hit musical Mamma Mia, is home to several breathtaking silk sand beaches bordered by bottle-green pine forests and lapped by glass-clear waters, including the best of the best Lalaria, a secret cove that can only be reached by boat. Take a walk along one of the 26 well-marked walking calderimi trails on the island if you're feeling energetic, or wander the cobblestoned streets of the main town. On Bourtzi, the capital's remarkably picturesque peninsula with a tiny Venetian castle, you can toast the end of your stay with a sunset cocktail.

Skiathos Mystery

This modest hotel in Skiathos Town checks all the right boxes thanks to its stylish suites, stunning rooftop views, and attentive service. What was the final straw? There is a pool there as well. The bars, stores, and restaurants of the harbor and Papadiamantis Street are a walkable third of a mile away (600 meters) from the property, which is tucked away on the outskirts of town. It also manages to be quiet while still being close to the action.

Elivi Skiathos

Hotel settings don't get more picturesque than this, with pink sunsets, shady pine trees, and views for miles. You can tell right away how the hotel is going to be when you step out onto the expansive terrace from the art-filled lobby: slick but not cold.

Skiathos Princess

There are many beach hotels on Skiathos, but few have a stretch of sand this impressive.

Despite being known as the island's favorite five-star hotel, the Princess is still a family-run labor of love and one of the best Greek island hotels available. Although the beachfront location may have already won you over, there are plenty of other reasons to visit, such as the excellent service, fun activities for kids, and chic interiors.

Danai Beach Resort, Halkidiki

One of the most opulent locations in Greece is without a doubt Danai Beach Resort, which boasts a private beach, an elaborate spa, and villas with sea views. The five-star retreat features a range of restaurants, is family-friendly, and has everything you need to keep your little ones entertained while you relax by the beach with a vinsanto in your hand.

Aristi Mountain Resort & Villa

The eco-friendly Aristi Mountain Resort doesn't have beach views, but its perch atop the verdant Pindus Mountains gives it the ideal haven for anyone looking for an opulent getaway from nature. You may embark on a hike through the Vikos Gorge, one of the deepest canyons in the world, just a few minutes from your door when you're not cuddled up in front of the lounge's crackling fireplace with a good book or unwinding in the spa's sauna.

Mr. and Mrs. White, of Paros

The peace of Mr. & Mrs. White in Paros is available to travelers of all kinds. The Cycladic structure was designed with simplicity in mind, and the colorful climbing bougainvilleas on it are a tribute to the traditional Greek village in which it is located. All bathrooms are filled with toiletries by Drops, a small boutique brand from Athens that uses natural olive and grape oils in its products. Each of the huge rooms has a very comfortable bed, a and large veranda, and all bathrooms contain toiletries.

Domes Noruz Chania, Autograph Collection

All travelers can find accommodations at the adults-only boutique Domes Noruz. There are six lodging options, each with a different set of experiences. The Domes Noruz Chania is the ultimate adult playground, offering everything from helicopter flights over the Samaria Gorge to moonlit live jazz.

Amanzoe and Port Heli

The magnificent Amanzoe is situated on the Peloponnese's east coast, surrounded by ancient olive groves. With its Greek mythology-inspired neoclassical architecture and the area's scattered UNESCO ruins, this building gives the impression that it is located on the modern-day Acropolis.

CHAPTER FOUR
Best places in Greece for couples: Romantic Greek islands, charming towns, and stunning cities
Lindos, Rhodes - for the Ideal Blend of Nature & History

- Explore beautiful coves and remote bays
- Travel to the Athena Lindia Temple
- Discover the old town's cobblestone alleys.

The three components that make a romantic vacation are abundant in Lindos on the Greek island of Rhodes. It offers first-rate lodging as well as breathtaking coves and bays, famous UNESCO sites, medieval cobblestone villages, and other fascinating places.

Since Rhodes is the largest of the Greek islands, it is ideal for a longer stay because it has a diverse landscape and several sizable towns.

Lindos is charming, built around bays, and has one of the biggest acropolises in Greece. It is only second in size to Rhodes Town.

The Temple of Athena Lindia on the top of the Acropolis made Lindos famous throughout the ancient Greek world. With its sandstone-colored ruins set against the Mediterranean Sea's sparkling sapphire, it is one of the most popular tourist destinations in the world. Along with its impressive Knights of St. John fortress, Lindos is well-known for its Roman and Byzantine ruins.

Three fantastic beaches are close by, so you can head there once you're done exploring Lindos' numerous ruins and winding through its tiny alleyways. One of the most beautiful beaches in the entire Greek archipelago, St. Paul's beach is secluded and excellent for snorkeling.

By night, Lindos comes to life with rooftop terrace bars, taverns by the beach, and secluded swim-up pool bars.

Ways to get there: Quick boat from Rhodes Town.

Staying places: If you want a romantic suite with a private pool and views of the sea, stay at the adults-only Lindos Grand Resort and Spa.

IOS is one of Greece's most romantic islands

- At Ios's idyllic beaches, you can swim and snorkel
- Experience Ios Chora's white-washed homes
- Go to Homer's Tomb on a pilgrimage.

Couples looking to unwind and have a romantic getaway should consider staying on Ios Island for a week. Despite its small size, the island has beautiful beaches where visitors can unwind and go snorkeling in the clear Greek waters. Visits to Homer's Tomb and the archeological site of Skarkos are two of the best things to do on Ios during the day.

Ios is one of the Aegean Sea's most romantic islands, but few people are aware of this. This is so because Ios is primarily recognized as the party-lovers sister island to Mykonos. In fact, during the months of July and August, university students from all over the world descend upon this small island for a live party. But once August is over, the island's tranquility returns and it becomes a haven for lovers.

Dinner by the port or in the town is a necessity for a special evening. Walking through Ios Chora's winding, white streets with your special someone as the sun sets over the sea is one of the most romantic things you can do. The actual windmills that give the island its notoriety can also be found at the top of the town.

Ways to get there: Ferry service direct from Athens (4-6 hrs).

Staying places: On Ios, the Yialos Ios Hotel is a fantastic choice for a romantic getaway at a reasonable price.

For windmills and iconic views, visit Santorini

- Take in the distinctive windmills and vibrant architecture
- Savor the breathtaking Oia sunset
- Obtain a taste of the wine and seafood that is available locally

With its azure waters, contrasting beaches, and recognizable white and blue Oia buildings, Santorini is renowned as one of the world's most romantic vacation spots.

Santorini is a wonderful romantic getaway year-round, even though the majority of visitors come in the summer. In the height of the tourist season, Oia can become congested despite being known for its breathtaking sunset photo opportunities. As an alternative, arrange a private sunset sail for the two of you to experience the most beautiful scenery.

Amoudi Bay and Red Sand Beach, two locations that ought to be on any Santorini itinerary, are beautiful places to stroll around in together.

Rent a beach chair and spend some time at Perissa Beach admiring the clear water and alluring black sand if the weather is warm.

The Heart of Santorini, a heart-shaped opening in a rock that overlooks the caldera just south of Amos Athiniós, is the ideal location for a romantic photo with your significant other. By scheduling a photography session, you can take advantage of the breathtaking scenery and create priceless memories that you will cherish for years to come.

The delicious Greek cuisine is best enjoyed over romantic dinners with a view of the setting sun, at a local winery's wine tasting, or while sipping a cocktail or coffee.

Ways to get there: Ferry service direct from Athens (2.5-5 hrs).

Staying places: Make reservations for a stay at the adults-only La Perla Villas and Suites in Oia, where you can treat yourself to a distinctive cave villa with your private pool overlooking the renowned caldera, for the height of luxury.

For a Romantic City Break, Visit Athens

- Spend the evening at a cozy rooftop bar or restaurant
- Discover Plaka's charming streets, markets, and tavernas
- Visit the world-class museums and archaeological sites in Athens to satisfy your curiosity

For anyone who enjoys culture and history and wants to take a romantic getaway in Greece, Athens, the country's capital and largest metropolis, is an obvious choice. The most discriminating travelers will find something exceptional in today's Athens, a city of hip rooftop bars, top-notch museums, and stunning boutique hotels.

The Acropolis, the Ancient Agora, and the Parthenon are among the must-see attractions in Athens that evoke the romance of Classical Athens. You can fully immerse yourself in Greek culture and make lasting memories by engaging in practical activities like taking a Greek cooking class, exploring the Varvakeios Agora Central Market, or enrolling in a dance lesson with Zorba Inside Me.

Explore the charming Plaka neighborhood's streets, take a stroll through the Diomedes Botanic Garden with your significant other, attend a late-night performance at the Odeon of Herodes Atticus, and climb Lycabettus Hill for the most romantic sunset views. One of the great cities in the world, Athens serves as the ideal setting for an epic romance.

Ways to get there: Get on a plane and fly to the airport in Athens.

Staying places: In Athens, there are numerous exquisite designer hotels. The elegant rooms at Shila Athens, which is located at the base of Lycabettus Hill, have a vintage feel and feature four-poster beds.

MONEMVASIA: A Charming Greek Castle-Village

- Take in the medieval architecture
- View the Aegean Sea in all its glory from the castle
- Sup on some local malvasia wine

Monemvasia, a town with a castle, is one of the most charming destinations in mainland Greece. Built on an islet connected to the mainland by a 200-meter-long bridge, this medieval settlement is in perfect condition. Monemvasia Castle is the perfect location for a memorable getaway for two. It resembles a stone ship built to withstand the ferocious winds and waves of the Aegean Sea.

One of the most romantic activities you can do with your significant other is to stroll through the cobblestone streets of this quaint Greek town, where no vehicles are permitted past its imposing gate. This is especially true in the evening when the bijou town is perfectly dimly lit.

For the most breathtaking views of the Aegean Sea that stretch as far as the eye can see, you must hike up to the Upper Town.

When you get back to Monemvasia's Lower Town, reward yourself with a bottle of the region's Malvasia wine at one of the charming bars.

Set your alarm for the early morning to witness what is arguably Greece's most magnificent sunrise for an experience you will never forget.

Ways to get there: From Athens, a car or bus (4 hrs).

Staying places: One-of-a-kind experiences can be had by sleeping inside the walls of a fortified medieval castle. So, reserve a room at the Byzantino Boutique Hotel while visiting Monemvasia to have the opportunity to stay in a historically significant and quaintly retro mansion that has been lovingly restored.

Halkidiki – for a Different Coastal Getaway

- Beaches with white sand are ideal for swimming
- Visit Aristotle's birthplace Stageira
- View Mount Athos' rocky beauty from a distance

Halkidiki is one of those places that will make you want to keep going back even though Greece as a whole is stunning. A stunning region made up of three peninsulas, sometimes referred to as "legs," that jut out into the Aegean Sea, Halkidiki is situated in the northern part of the country just a few hours' drive from the vibrant city of Thessaloniki.

The western leg is the most well-liked, filled with chic hotels, bars, and eateries ideal for couples seeking a glitzy beach getaway. The eastern leg, Mount Athos, contains a closed monastery where visitors are prohibited, and the middle leg is more serene and rural.

Due to its extensive, beautiful coastline, which features white beaches for lounging, turquoise waters for diving and snorkeling, and secluded bays for exploring, Halkidiki is the ideal destination for a romantic getaway.

Due to its accessibility, there is no shortage of accommodations that are suitable for couples, ranging from charming boutique hotels with views of the ocean to lavish resorts with numerous pools and secluded beaches.

There are plenty of historical sites, such as Stageira, the birthplace of the famous philosopher Aristotle who famously wrote about love with phrases like "two people find in each other's virtues-one soul and two bodies," as well as opportunities for hiking through lush pine forests and along coastal paths, for those who like to keep busy.

Ways to get there: Vehicle or bus from Thessaloniki (1 hr).

Staying places: The middle peninsula's Porto Carras Meliton Grand Resort has a private beach, three pools, a spa, a golf course, a marina, half a dozen bars and restaurants, and even a bowling alley in addition to its roomy accommodations with views of the ocean.

- Purchase items made locally
- Dine on regional food at the Watermill of Zia café
- Visit a nearby country estate and partake in a wine-and-oil tasting there

There are so many incredible places for a romantic getaway in Greece, but if you're looking for something off the beaten path, consider visiting the mountain village of Zia.

Kos, a Greek island, has a small village named Zia. Its precise location is close to Mount Dikaios's base, Kos's tallest peak. It is a remarkably lovely location that is ideal for couples who value nature.

You can enjoy a variety of activities and wonderful ways to spend quality time with your loved ones here. Walking down the cobblestone streets and perusing the handmade goods is one of the best things for couples to do in Zia. You can visit many incredible art galleries and boutiques that specialize in handmade jewelry.

Visit the cafe at the Watermill of Zia if you want to eat the best tzatziki on Kos. In addition to having the best food, this location has the best sunset views over Zia.

You ought to stay all day at Kos Natural Park to fully appreciate the breathtaking scenery. This is a great way to stay away from the crowds and enjoy the stunning Island views. Zia is a great starting point for exploring many other Kos regions.

The visit to a winery is one vacation that is highly advised for couples. A romantic afternoon spent together would be ideal at one of the Island's many vineyards, which all have gorgeous scenery and excellent regional wines.

Ways to get there: 30-minute drive plus a 50-minute direct flight from Athens.

Staying places: The most incredible lodging options in Kos, particularly for couples, can be found in Zia. You can locate the ideal residence regardless of your financial constraints. For the best garden views and to experience genuine Greek hospitality at its finest, check out Orea Ellas Kos - Deluxe Residences.

In the winter, KASTORIA is the most romantic city in Greece

- Enjoy the old-world charm of the Ottoman architecture
- Romantic stroll along the lakefront promenade
- Enjoy chilly temperatures all year long

Kastoria is one of Greece's most picturesque cities, but there isn't much foreign tourism there. While most people don't consider northern Greece when planning a romantic getaway, this region is much more tranquil than the islands and is filled with charming lakes and mountains.

The city is a cute collection of historic homes, Byzantine churches, cobblestone streets, and cafes. It is a picturesque and romantic city that is encircled by Lake Orestiada and has the Grammos and Vitsi mountains in the distance. Kastoria is a great summer destination in Greece when the islands are hot and teeming with tourists because it doesn't experience mass tourism and summer temperatures don't often exceed 30C.

Kastoria is a small city, but there is still a lot to do there for couples:

- Esplanade by the lake and stroll there
- Explore the historic Doltso and Apozari neighborhoods' cobblestone streets.
- Visit Panagia Mavriotissa to see the Byzantine murals.
- For stunning city views, hike to Profit Ilias Church.
- Visit Dragon's Cave to see stalactites and underground lakes.
- Get a coffee or frappe at one of the lakeside cafes on Meg Alexandrou
- Investigate the Korean abandoned villages.
- For an afternoon, drive to Nymfaio, the Switzerland of northern Greece.

By car or private transfer, Kastoria is reachable from Meteora and has a good bus service to Thessaloniki.

Ways to get there: Vehicle or bus from Thessaloniki (2-3 hrs).

Staying places: The atmosphere and warm hospitality of the local owners will encourage you to stay at Vergoula's Mansion. Located in the center of the city, it is a lovely, traditional mansion with stunning views. The price includes a hearty Greek breakfast.

For spiritual couples, check out Metaora

- Take in the spiritual beauty of the six Meteora Monasteries
- View the monolithic rock formations while eating some of the local cuisines
- Start hiking along 20 km of beautiful trails

One of Greece's most stunning sights is Meteora, which is composed of sandstone peaks topped with hidden monasteries and shrouded in the morning fog. Along with being one of the oldest UNESCO World Heritage listings, it is also the largest archaeological landscape in the nation.

The first settlers of Meteora were monks who came here in search of seclusion and pious solitude beginning in the 14th century. The monasteries and cave chapels they constructed were only reachable by ropes and ladders, which is reflected in their precarious locations. Ironically, a location created by hermits with a solitary retreat in mind has evolved into one of the top honeymoon destinations in Greece.

Even though Meteora is frequently visited as a day trip, the region naturally lends itself to a longer stay, especially for those seeking a tranquil, atmospheric escape from the larger cities. Excellent lodging and dining options are available in Kalabaka Town, many of which have breathtaking views of the "columns of the sky."

On various days of the week, six of the 24 monasteries are open to the public. Staying in Meteora for at least a few nights will be necessary if you want to see them all. It is worthwhile to visit as many monasteries as you can because each one has a distinct personality and is connected by common architectural elements like charming cloisters and lovely rose gardens.

The area's hills and valleys are traversed by 14 interconnected hiking trails totaling 20 km, which provide sweeping views of the monasteries and the mysterious rock formations.

Ways to get there: Using a car, bus, or day tour from Thessaloniki, travel time is 2.5 to 3 hours.

Staying places: An excellent starting point for exploring Meteora is Kalabaka town, which is only a short drive from the monasteries. The opulent old-world decor of Hotel Doupiani House surpasses even the views for an unforgettable experience of waking up among the rocks.

Nafplio is one of Greece's most picturesque towns

- Explore Byzantine churches and Neoclassical building styles
- Views can be seen from Palamidi Castle
- Take a boat to the Venetian fortress Bourtzi

One of the most romantic places in the nation, Nafplio (Nafplion), the charming coastal town that served as the first capital of the modern Greek state, is regarded by locals as such. The historical old town is a labyrinth of paved streets bordered by bougainvillea, with a castle floating in the harbor and a medieval Venetian fortress perched atop a hill above.

One of Greece's prettiest towns is only a two-hour drive from Athens, and there are plenty of activities for couples in this town.

Spend the day relaxing at a nearby beach, stroll along the harbor at dusk, or take a boat ride to see the underwater Bourtzi Castle. Try the local wine while spending the evenings at the eateries and bars that line the square. If you enjoy history, you can spend a lot of time exploring the top-notch museums in Nafplio while learning about the contributions made by the Venetians, Franks, Ottomans, and Greeks.

Spend an entire morning ascending to the Palamidi Fortress, then strolling along the walls to take in the breathtaking views of the town and the sea. Ancient ruins and even more breathtaking views can be found on Nafplio's acropolis, the Akronafplia.

The Peloponnese can be easily explored from Nafplio, which is a good starting point if you want to travel further because it is home to many ancient sites.

Ways to get there: From Athens, a car or bus (2-3 hrs).

Staying places: Consider staying at the Nafsimedon Hotel, a boutique establishment with tastefully furnished rooms and a lovely courtyard in the middle of everything.

Kefalonia is Known for its Colorful Architecture and Sea Caves

- The limestone caves can be explored by boat
- Observe wild sea turtles
- Visit a vineyard and savor some regional wines

Since Kefalonia is the biggest island in Greece, it makes the ideal setting for a getaway with your significant other. Between Fiskardo in the north, where you can rent a boat and explore the coves, and Skala in the south, where the golden sand beaches offer a haven for relaxation. To fully experience the island's many distinctive and varied regions, renting a car is the ideal mode of transportation.

Sea turtles can be seen attempting to snag scraps from fishing boats as you take a morning stroll along the harbor in Argostoli. Go on a wine tour and then have dinner at one of the many romantic outdoor restaurants in Kampana Square. Or, the most famous vantage point on the entire island, Myrtos Beach, offers paragliding for couples who are feeling particularly daring.

Take a moment to explore the Drogatari cave beneath Athens, or go to Melissani cave at noon to see how the setting sun illuminates the opening of the cave lake. Both of these activities will help you cool off from the heat of the Greek sun.

Ways to get there: From Patras, you can take a direct ferry or a one-hour flight to Athens (3 hrs).

Staying places: Stay in Lassi to be close to the city's center and to explore the region's breathtaking wonders. White Rocks is an elegant beachfront hotel in the area.

For couples who enjoy partying, MYKONOS is one of the best places in Greece

- indulge excessively at Mykonos' renowned beach parties and bars
- On Agrari Beach and Ornus Beach, you can find quiet swimming areas
- In Mykonos Old Town, stroll around the whitewashed homes

Mykonos is renowned for its exotic and extravagant beach parties, making it the best Greek island for young couples and the ideal destination for those who love to savor the nightlife. The picturesque Old Town of Mykonos, with its whitewashed houses and blue doors, and its well-known windmills provide a magical and romantic setting unmatched by any other.

Going on a sunset cruise in Mykonos, which is renowned for its beautiful sunsets, is the best thing to do there for a romantic getaway. Due to their lively beach parties and upbeat atmosphere, the Paradise and Super Paradise beaches are well-liked by couples. Here, throughout the summer, a lot of well-known DJs perform live. Couples seeking a more private experience amidst breathtaking nature should visit one of the less popular, more remote beaches like Agrari Beach or Ornus Beach.

Mykonos is simultaneously enchanting, mysterious, glamorous, and magical. This Greek Aegean Island is not only the best for honeymoons, but it's also a great place to celebrate anniversaries or just take a beach vacation with your significant other.

Mykonos' peak season is from June to September, so make sure to reserve your hotel far in advance.

Ways to get there: Direct flights from Athens take 45 minutes, and ferries take 2.5–4 hours.

Staying places: wonderful hotel with ocean views, a spa, and a private beach is Psarou Beach.

For couples who appreciate history, visit Rhodes Old Town

- Discover Rhodes Old Town, which is listed as a UNESCO World Heritage Site
- Pay a visit to the magnificent Palace of the Grand Masters
- Find the charming restaurant of your choice

Greece's Old Town of Rhodes, a UNESCO World Heritage Site, has cobbled streets reminiscent of Game of Thrones and is the ideal destination for a romantic getaway. Experiencing distinctive luxury doesn't have to be expensive.

The Old Town of Rhodes, which was named a UNESCO World Heritage Site in 1988, is renowned for being one of the oldest "living Old Towns" in Europe, which means that people continue to live and conduct business within its historic walls.

The Palace of the Grand Masters is the island's crowning achievement and a must-visit for anyone who wants to learn more about the past of Old Rhodes. When the Catholic Military Order, the Knights Hospitaller, took possession of the island in 1309, the castle that had been constructed as a castle in the 7th century was transformed into an administrative center.

Alternately, begin your stroll here on top of the castle walls for stunning views of Turkey that are framed by the Old Town's mosques and minarets.

Ways to get there: From Athens, a direct flight (1 hr.).

Staying places: A quiet, medieval Knight's Mansion that has been painstakingly transformed into a boutique hotel with six opulent suites is Kokkini Porta Rossa, the first structure you see as you enter St. John's Gate. From the wooden balcony's nifty roof, make a Romeo and Juliet-style proposal.

The Pelion Peninsula: A Hidden Treasure for Spouses in Greece

- Immersed in the romance and myth of Mount Pelion
- Enroll in a farm-to-table cooking course
- To locate serene pebble beaches, take the backroads

The Pelion Peninsula is without a doubt one of Greece's most romantic locations. This region, which can be found in Thessaly on the Greek mainland, is renowned for its untamed beauty. There are beautiful green-blue hidden coves, dense forests, pebbly beaches, and excellent hiking opportunities here.

Mount Pelion commands the entire scene. Greek mythology states that the Centaurs called this mountain their home. The Jason and the Argonauts tale, in which Jason and his crew embark on a heroic quest to steal a golden fleece from a dragon that never sleeps, is the most well-known tale about Pelion.

According to legend, wood from the forests of Pelion was used to construct the boat. Many marriages, including those between Pileas and Thetis and King Perithos and Ippodamea, reportedly took place at Pelion, according to Greek mythology. Even today, many Greeks still want to get married to Pelion because of this.

Most importantly, the Pelion Peninsula has not yet attracted the attention of the general public, making it a wonderful location for romantic getaways. The numerous lovely traditional tavernas and adorable little villages on Pelion are where you can learn about authentic Greek culture.

To experience everything, the peninsula has to offer, traveling together is the best option. Beach hopping along Pelion's eastern coast, taking a cooking class with a friend at Karaikos Farm in Portaria, and visiting a winery near Argalasti should all be high on your list of must-dos.

Pelion is home to a plethora of romantic eateries, but a few recommendations are Tsipouradiko Flokos in the city of Volos, Aggellika fish taverna in Mylopotamos, El Resto Bar in Mouresi, Victoria Cafe in Damouchari, and Aggellika in Mouresi.

Ways to get there: Thessaloniki or Athens by car/bus (3.5 hours) (4.5 hrs).

Staying places: Three hotels that are suggested for couples are Hotel Des Roses in Platanias, Sunrise Tsagarada in Tsagarada, and Katerina Fotopoulos Rooms and Apartments at Papa Nero Beach.

Planning tips for the ideal Greek honeymoon trip for couples

During the off-season, go to Greece. Visit Greece outside of the busy summer months for the best chance of discovering a quiet swimming cove or having a mountain hiking trail to yourself. Ideal times to visit are in the spring (April/May) and fall (September/October).

Your trip should be organized around a significant anniversary. Plan your trip to coincide with an anniversary or another noteworthy calendar date to make your vacation extra special.

Try to find a remote area. A balanced itinerary should include both more remote locations and popular islands or large cities. If you want to experience a popular day trip location (like Meteora) without the crowds, sometimes it's as simple as staying there overnight or for a couple of days.

Make reservations for logistics like airport transfers. Before you leave, arrange your basic logistics to prevent hassles (and potential conflict) while you're traveling.

In advance, make your hotel reservations. especially if your trip is during the summer.

Invest in a better room. From a double to a suite, excellent lodging can become something spectacular.

Mix up the activities you plan so that there is something for both you and your partners. A mix of culture, history, outdoor recreation, and relaxation is desirable in your destination.

Think about getting a rental car. You'll be able to travel more freely and on your schedule as a result of this. Additionally, you will have more time to bond with each other in the car. On Local Rent, locate a fantastic rental car deal.

Schedule special meals at restaurants. If you want to always have something to look forward to, sprinkle your schedule with a few memorable dining occasions.

Spend the extra money on a few special occasions. There is no better way to create lasting memories with your partner in Greece than to hire a photographer for the day or spend a little more on a private tour.

CHAPTER FIVE
Most Beautiful Cities to Visit in Greece

Athens

Visitors visiting Greece on vacation usually stay in Athens. Visitors from North America and Northern Europe usually make their initial stop at its airport. They then fly off for their sun and sand getaway after a quick tour of the Acropolis and the Plaka neighborhood.

Visit the majestic Acropolis, a landmark of the city and the nation, which is home to the Parthenon temple and the commanding Caryatids. You can purchase a single ticket that gives you access to the Athens Acropolis, the Ancient Agora, the Kerameikos Archaeological Museum, Hadrian's Library, and more. Don't miss the new Acropolis Museum with its cutting-edge design and priceless treasures, and be sure to stop by the Odeon of Herodes Atticus as well.

Thessaloniki

Thessaloniki is among the best cities in Greece for a city getaway. It is regarded as Greece's second capital, or better yet, the capital of Northern Greece. With a wealth of attractions, many of which are conveniently accessible and close to one another, and a variety of cuisines to try, it provides the ideal urban yet cosmopolitan vacation destination.

The renowned White Tower, a tower constructed in the 15th century as a fortress and prison during the Ottoman occupation, is the city's most well-known feature. It is now one of the locations that both locals and tourists alike visit frequently because it houses the Thessaloniki City Museum. The observation tower is the best place to go for stunning images and sweeping panoramas of the coastal city.

The historic waterfront, often called "Palia Paralia," is located to the east of the White Tower. Take a stroll and take in the historic architecture that can be seen from Nikis Avenue and White Tower to the Harbor. The New Waterfront, a contemporary promenade and a favorite gathering place for young people, couples, locals, and tourists, is located close to the White Tower.

Volos

Volos, a lovely city that blends mountains and the sea, is located in the regional entity of Magnesia. The magnificent Sporades islands are close by and are located across the Pagasetic Gulf.

In Volos, you may stroll down the promenade and take in a breathtaking sunset, or you can explore the town and shop on Ikonomiki Street or Ermou Street. There are several tsipouradika where you may get a drink and have fun.

Pilio, a village on the Mountain Pelion with traditional homes, breathtaking scenery, and a choice of hiking trails to experience unspoiled nature, is a perfect day trip from Volos. Visit the Manas Spring in Portaria or stroll along the Centaur Path. You can also ride the Moutzouris Steam Train.

Pelion is not only a hilly region but also home to some beautiful beaches, such as Mylopotamos, Agios Ioannis, and Fakistra, where you can weave.

Ioannina

Another one of Greece's top cities is Ioannina, also spelled Giannena, and noted for its vibrant city life. Built upon the shores of the stunning Lake Pamvotida, the city is lovely and snug in the winter and bustling and alive in the summer.

By strolling around the lake of Pamvotida under the gorgeous promenade's stout plane trees, you may explore it. You can also take a boat tour to visit the island that is in the middle of the lake and to tour the lake itself. Numerous attractions, including wall paintings of religious figures and old temples, can be found there.

The oldest Byzantine fortification in Greece, Ioannina, is the first place to see in the Ioannina core. In the several museums housed within the castle town, you may learn everything there is to know about the history of the city. Visit the Aslan Passa Mosque, the Municipal Ethnographic Museum, and the Silversmithing Museum.

Other things to do in Ioannina:

- Perama Cave exploration

- Try some of the regional food of Epirus
- Go to the Dodoni Theatre and Sanctuary
- Explore Old Town on foot
- Enjoy cocktails in bars with live music

Chania

With a population of over 156,000 people, Chania is one of the best cities in Greece, located this time in the south on the island of Crete. It is a significant seaside island city. The majority of the island's nicest beaches may be found in the Chania area, which also offers lively nightlife, a youthful vibe, and other attractions.

Head to the Old Venetian Harbour, where there is a magnificent promenade by the water, and stop by the Maritime Museum of Crete or the Archaeological Museum to get a sense of Chania's distinctive ambiance. The Firka Venetian Fortress, a Maritime Museum and a beautiful sight to behold are close by. Wander the streets and take in the vibrant inhabitants. Eat some of the local specialties; it's a wonderful food.

Outside of the municipal limits, the area around Chania is home to magnificent landscapes, untamed settings with cyan-colored waves, and fantastic beaches and coves. Don't pass on exploring the adjacent Balos Lagoon, regarded as one of the top beaches in the world, for its stunning beauty. Elafonisi, renowned for its unending dunes, clean lakes, and untamed landscape, is another place you shouldn't forget.

Kavala

Northern Greece's Kavala is a coastal city centered on a bay with a marina. The city of Kavala is bustling with activity in a variety of neighborhoods and parks, and it has a sizable student population.

Visit the majestic Kavala castle in Old Town, which has the best vistas of the entire city, to immerse yourself in it. You can take pictures there or just gaze in awe at what's in front of you. On the way back, stroll through the Old Town areas and take in the charming houses.

Visit the Mehmet Ali statue on a horse that is located in front of his former home, which is now a museum. Walk to the Old Lighthouse for more expansive city views and take in the vista from above.

Other things to do in Kavala:

- Travel to the Halil Bey Mosque
- Visit the Mehmed Ali Imaret
- Go to the Kavala Archaeological Museum
- Check out the Tobacco Museum

Kastoria

Kastoria is another enchanted city in Greece. The beautiful city of Kastoria is constructed as an amphitheater with a view of Lake Orestiada between the Grammos and Vitsi mountains on a small peninsula.

Given that it serves as a natural habitat for numerous threatened and endangered plant and animal species, the lake is lovely and well worth a trip for nature enthusiasts. The Dragon's Cave, which has a lot of stalactites to examine, is located nearby the lake.

Visit Agios Athanasios viewpoint for breathtaking views of the city, the lake, and the surrounding rocky terrain. You can also hop on a tour boat that cruises around the lake and the peninsula, offering you a chance to see something no one else will see, depending on the time of year.

Visit any of the 60 Byzantine churches that were built in Kastoria's core to learn more about the city's long Byzantine heritage, which dates back to the ninth century. Visit places like the church of Doltso and Agios Panteleimonas, and the Panagia Mavriotissa Monastery beside the lake, to name a few. Visit the Byzantine Art Museum at Dexameni Square to discover more about the rich heritage.

Nafplio

Nafplion served as the new state's initial capital when it was created. The most charming and romantic city still exudes the magnificence of that period. It is the ideal weekend retreat because it is situated in the Peloponnese, only two hours from Athens.

To reach the tall Palamidi Fortress, erected with bastions during the 18th century, ascend the 999 stairs (as is said to be the case). From up there, you have a wonderful view of the city, the limitless sea, and the Bourtzi stronghold.

Take a boat to the islet of Bourtzi to explore its fascinating history, or visit the Akronapflia Fortress, another castle with breathtaking views. Alternately, enjoy a stroll down the beach Promenade of Arvanitia, which has rugged cliffs on one side and the sea on the other. It is a kilometer long and ideal for a romantic evening at sunset.

Other activities in Nafplion include:

Explore the Archaeological Museum

Visit Syntagma Square and sip coffee

At Antica Gelateria di Roma, indulge in the best gelato

Float on Karathonas Beach

Walk around the Old Town and purchase mementos

Kalamata

Kalamata, in the heart of Messinia, is another one of Greece's top cities. It produces olive oil, raisins, and other premium goods thanks to its natural resources and fertile soil.

The "Castle of Isabeau" on the Farai Acropolis, which serves as the city's landmark and is where the yearly International Dance Festival is held each year in front of a large crowd, is a well-known landmark. Visit the

Archaeological Museum of Messinia, which houses artifacts from numerous adjacent ancient settlements, to gain a better understanding of the area's past.

Visit the renowned Byzantine church of the Holy Apostles and the Cathedral of Ypapantis while strolling through the Old Town beneath the castle for vistas of the neoclassical homes and the grandeur of the architecture.

You may easily take a trip to the Mani peninsula from Kalamata, which is a spectacular area of unspoiled beauty, rocky beaches, and crystal-clear seawater. The travel takes up to 2 hours and is approximately 100 kilometers away. There, you can explore Areopoli or Limeni, awe at the magnificence of Cape Tenaro, or go to the Diros Caves.

Xanthi

The city of Xanthi is a vibrant destination that is packed with history, art, tradition, and nature. It is situated at the base of the Rhodopi mountain range in Thrace, Northern Greece.

Any type of traveler can find a variety of ways to experience the city's spirit. You can immerse yourself in Xanthi's distinctive charm by taking a stroll through the Old Town.

The Folk and History Museum of Xanthi, the Public Paint Gallery, and the contemporary art museum "The House of Shadow" are then good places to start your museum trip.

The Nestos River and the Nestos Straits offer freshwater swimming and outdoor sports for nature enthusiasts and explorers.

Trikala

Without a doubt, Trikala is one of the nicest cities in Greece for both tourists and residents. It is a winter wonderland in the Thessaly region, especially for its Christmas town, but it is worth a trip any time of the year.

The town's famed Clock Tower and the 600-year-old Kastro are both in plain sight. Visit the well-known Matsopoulos Mill monument by the river for a chance to study Trikala, or go for a fun and cost-free bike ride throughout the city.

The stone-arched bridges over the Lithaios River near Trikala, including the Stone Bridge Gate and the Stone Bridge of Palaiokarya, are indisputable landmarks.

The most alluring aspect is its proximity to Meteora, a popular Greek tourist destination where you may marvel at "soaring" granite masses with monasteries erected on top; that's a sight to see and remember. Only 29 minutes away, Meteora is located 26 kilometers to the northwest of Trikala.

Preveza

Preveza is one of the top cities in Greece and is located in the same region of Epirus as Ioannina. This city provides a wide range of choices. It was built by the sea, at the so-called Ambracian Gulf, which is famous for its delectable shrimp.

You can go on a promenade stroll and take in the mild weather, eat delectable food or seafood, or go sightseeing in the adjacent areas. You might start with Nicopolis, whose ruins were left in situ despite being an old city that was constructed in 31 B.C.

Alternately, a few kilometers outside of Acheron River Springs is where you can go swimming or rafting.

Other things to do in Preveza:

Around-the-Acheron River hike

Take a dip at Alonaki Beach.

Visiting Lichnos Beach

Best Places to Go Hiking in Greece

Parnitha Mountain, Athens

With a peak elevation of over 4,500 feet, Parnitha is the highest mountain in Attica. It's the ideal hike for a day trip from Athens because it's only about 90 minutes away by car and has a variety of routes.

You could choose to bike or walk along parts of designated trails. As well as being popular, climbing has a cable car that takes visitors to the summit.

The forests of Parnitha Mountain are covered in pine trees, home to about 30 different species of animals. Of the 800 or so different kinds of herbs and plants that grow here, deer, rabbits, and foxes are the most prevalent.

One of the best mountains in Greece, Parnitha Mountain, is dotted with numerous exquisite churches and monasteries, such as Aghia Triada, Kleiston Monastery, and Agios Kyprianos Monastery, which conveniently mark some of the region's fantastic hiking trails.

The Panos Cave, located close to the ruins of the Filis Fortress from the fourth century BC in Western Parnitha, is another noteworthy location. To see the stalagmites and stalactites that have been decorated in the cave, you must ascend a fairly challenging pass through a gorge.

Lycabettus Hill, Athens

The breathtaking views of Athens that await you at the top of Lycabettus Hill make it arguably the best urban hike in Greece. The highest hill in Athens, Lycabettus, rises over 900 feet above the city to the northwest of the Acropolis.

Along the zigzagging path to the summit, pass numerous green cactus, pine trees, and other native shrubs. The extraordinary views over Athens, which extend as far as the Saronic Gulf beyond the port of Piraeus, make the short hike worthwhile.

At the top of the hill is the 1870 structure known as the Holy Church of Saint George, which is whitewashed.

Samaria Gorge, Crete

The stunning White Mountains National Park of Crete is home to the Samaria Gorge trail, which is located outside of Chania. Samaria Gorge is regarded as not only one of the best hikes in Greece but also among the most breathtaking hiking locations in all of Europe.

The trail descends from the plateau beneath the mountains to a secluded beach on the Aegean, traversing a 10-mile canyon—the longest gorge in Greece.

Rising rock formations can be seen in the mighty gorge. The path weaves across a shallow, rock-strewn river, measuring roughly 10 feet wide at its narrowest point and almost 500 feet wide at its widest. Be aware of the mountain goats of Samaria, which are frequently seen grazing on the dense bushes or bounding between rocks.

This UNESCO-protected Biosphere Reserve is home to an astounding 450 different species of plants and animals, including 70 that are endemic to Crete.

One of Samaria Gorge's highlights is the fragrance of pine, cypress, and holly trees. There are also several freshwater springs, abandoned villages, and churches.

Mount Eros, Hydra

The 12-mile Mount Eros loop on Hydra, a picturesque island, is one of the more difficult hikes in Greece. Based on your level of fitness and the number of stops you make; the entire lap takes about six hours.

As you climb the mountain to reach the summit, you will pass scenes of dry-stone walls that crisscross the grassy hillside and take in views of the Peloponnese and the Aegean Sea.

Lindos Acropolis, Rhodes

One of Rhodes' most attractive ancient towns is Lindos, making it among the best locations on the island to go hiking. The town's east coast Acropolis, which shines on a clifftop dotted with olive and cypress trees and overlooks the azure Aegean Sea, is the main attraction.

Starting in the charming old town of Lindos, take this short but hilly hike. Reach the fortress walls that encircle this post-Hellenic Acropolis by ascending a flight of stairs through the whitewashed buildings.

When you reach the top of Lindos Acropolis, you can explore the many ancient Greek ruins there, like the Byzantine chapel of Saint John and the goddess Athena Lindia's temple from the fourth century BC. The tall Doric columns are the most striking feature.

Skaros Rock, Santorini

One of Greece's most exhilarating hiking destinations is the volcanic island of Santorini. From Fira, the island's capital of whitewashed buildings, consider a headland hike. To reach Skaros Rock, which is about three miles away along a designated walking trail, start from Santorini's charming old harbor.

Climb the zigzagging Karavolades Stairs to give your lower body a good workout. On the trail, beware of donkey trains that might pass you by. Observe the Church of Saint Gerasimos and the Three Bells of Fira Church, two iconic Greek structures with gleaming turquoise domes.

An ancient castle's ruins and impressive rock formations can be found on Skaros Rock, a rocky outcrop. In the village of Imerovigli, where you have a variety of restaurants to choose from, reward your efforts with a mouthwatering mezze platter and a cool beverage.

Mount Olympus National Park, Thessaloniki

The mythical home of the gods, the mighty Mount Olympus, rises majestically to a height of 9,570 feet, making it the highest mountain in Greece and one of the best hikes in all of Europe.

Mount Olympus, which is close to the Gulf of Thérmai, is frequently covered in snow and occasionally has a cloud cover. This stunning hiking area features rivers and waterfalls, wooded canyons, green-covered hills, and isolated villages.

Mount Olympus National Park has 20 hiking routes that range in difficulty and length, and it has been a UNESCO Biosphere Reserve since 1981. Choose the simple, two-hour hike from Prionia to the Monastery of Agios Dionysios via Agios Spilaio.

One of the highlights is the charming Enipea waterfall and its sparkling pool, which can be found before navigating the Enipea River on a shaky wooden bridge in the direction of Agio Spilaio.

The Greek Orthodox monastery ruins are situated at the Enipeas ravine, tucked away in a forest of emerald hues. It was constructed in 1542, and during World War II, it was partially destroyed.

The mountain and its foothills are home to large carnivores like the brown bear and wolf, as well as roe deer, wild boar, and even wild boar. However, you're more likely to see the Balkan chamois, a member of the goat-antelope family, which can be seen in the summer on the alpine-like slopes.

Nea Kameni Island, Santorini

Another stunning hiking destination is the tiny, uninhabited island of Nea Kameni, which is located in the caldera of Santorini. The island, which is largely deserted aside from a few sprigs of Mediterranean shrubs, was created by volcanic eruptions that occurred between 1701 and 1711 and are still active today.

From the mainland, you can take the quick ferry to Nea Kameni and hike the strenuous trails through Nea Kameni Volcanic Park, which promises breathtaking views of Santorini's towering, red-and-black cliffs and whitewashed villages scattered across the top.

Mountain Skopos, Zakynthos

On the island of Zakynthos in the Ionian Sea's southeast, there is a nearly eight-mile moderately difficult mountain hike.

This four-hour hike starts close to the seaside town of Argassi. Explore the Panagia Skopiotissa Monastery and the Byzantine Church of St. Nikolaos Megalomatis. The monastery is the oldest church on the island, having been built in 1624.

Mount Skopos' typically dry terrain offers an educational hike with breathtaking views of the Ionian Sea and Zakynthos National Marine Park.

Balos Lagoon, Crete

Balos Lagoon, located on the northwest tip of Crete, offers hikers a tranquil experience that is typical of hiking in Greece. To experience the breathtaking views of the glistening lagoon and Gramvousa Island, start your hike from the hills above Balos Beach.

Follow the dry-dirt trail that descends from the mountainside to the ocean. Due to its soft sand and clear waters, Balos Beach is one of the best beaches in Greece. Bring a towel and your swimming suit so you can cool off in the tranquil lagoon after your hike.

Tomb of Cleobulus, Rhodes

This two-hour walk in Lindos, Rhodes, takes you from Lindos Beach northeast along a three-mile stretch of the coastal path. This is a quiet hike on a less-traveled path that goes in the opposite direction of the bustling town of Lindos.

Tomb of Cleobulus, a poet from Greece who lived in Lindos in the sixth century BC, but also one of the best places to see the Lindos Acropolis. Since there are no facilities along the way, stock up on supplies at the beach kiosk before you start walking.

Marathonisi Island National Marine Park, Zakynthos

In Zakynthos' Laganas Bay, the protected Marathonisi Island is well known for being a breeding ground for the critically endangered monk seal and a nesting location for endangered loggerhead sea turtles.

A stunning, creamy-colored beach with clear water can be found at the northern tip of this undeveloped island, which is covered in a lush pine, olive, and green oak forest. In addition, there are two sea caves southwest of the island where you can swim, kayak, or take in from a boat.

CHAPTER SIX
Best Things to Do in Greece

Greece, which is surrounded by the Ionian, Aegean, and Mediterranean seas and is situated in the Balkans, has a ton to offer visitors. Ancient temples and ruins will satisfy your historical fix. Local foods like tomatoes and olive oil will satisfy your culinary needs. The beach will satisfy your need for relaxation. Everyone can find something on land or at sea.

Tour the Acropolis

A visit to the Acropolis is essential. The Parthenon, the Erechtheion, the Propylaea, and the temple of Athena can all be seen from the ancient citadel, where you can also get sweeping views of Athens. Visit the Acropolis Museum to discover more about its past.

Take an authentic cooking class (Athens)

Anywhere in Greece is a good place to take a culinary class, but Athens boasts a wide variety of kitchens. The Greek Kitchen and CookinAthens both teach how to make traditional foods like moussaka and spanakopita, and Ergon House is an excellent choice for more daring diners who want to try things like chicken in puff pastry with gruyere and truffle.

Climb Mount Olympus

If you enjoy Greek mythology, Mount Olympus should not be skipped from your schedule. It is arguably one of the most famous mountains in the world.

As you ascend, you might picture the legends associated with Mount Olympus, which is recognized in Greek mythology as the site of Hades' control over the Underworld and the location where Zeus sat on his throne.

Sip famous white wines (Santorini)

Assyrtiko, a native grape of the island, as well as the Greek athiri and aidani varietals, are used to make the famous white wines from Santorini. There are numerous wine-tasting opportunities available for visitors thanks to the island of Santorini's numerous wineries, including Santo Winery, Venetsanos Winery, and Gavalas Winery (many with waterfront views, of course).

Taste tomatoes at the Tomato Industrial Museum (Santorini)

Visit the Tomato Industrial Museum in Santorini to learn how the island's small-fruited tomatoes acquire their distinctively sweet flavor. Learn about the conventional techniques for tomato production, processing, and gardening as you stroll through the former factory.

Uncover Lake Plastira

Greece, a country renowned for its abundance of natural beauty, is unique in that it has Lake Plastira, which is exceptional. Although it doesn't lessen its impressiveness, the fact that this lake is artificial distinguishes it from others. Canoeing, rafting, horseback riding, and hiking are all permitted on the lake's surrounding pathways, which are framed by oak and chestnut trees. The Greek district of Larditsa contains Lake Plastira, which provides an afternoon of adventure.

Admire the architecture in Santorini

Santorini, also called the island of Thira, is a honeymooner's paradise and one of the most stunning destinations on Earth. It is where couples go to get away from it all. The Greek Island of Santorini is renowned for its picture-postcard beauty, with its whitewashed traditional Cycladic buildings that sparkle in the blazing sun and contrast gorgeously with the deep blue waters and churches. Since the island's geography is made up of a volcano crater, you can expect to see some of the most breathtaking views in all of Greece while exploring the island's stunning architecture.

Shop your heart out in Little Venice (Mykonos)

Mykonos Town offers several attractions, including windmills, outdoor dining options, and a vibrant nightlife, but shopping in Little Venice is an unquestionable (and practically mandatory) must-do. According to UNESCO, the cobblestone commercial area is reminiscent of the Italian city that explorer Marco Polo called home and which served as a significant trading hub on the Silk Road to Asia, as the name of the area suggests. Little Venice is now a one-stop shop for all your necessities, including white dresses, honey jars, and evil eye necklaces.

Visit the Delphi

Aside from being one of Greece's top tourist destinations, Delphi has the distinction of being a UNESCO World Heritage Site.

Delphi, which is located on the slopes of Mount Parnassus, was formerly a well-known pilgrimage site for people who came there to pay respects to Apollo, the ancient Greek god of healing, music, light, and prophecy. Temples, a spectacular stadium, a theater, and charming historical ruins may all be seen in the area that was once frequented by followers who came to ask the Delphine Oracle for advice.

A nice spot to visit if you want to escape the city and discover another part of Greece is Delphi, which is located around 180 kilometers from the country's capital city of Athens.

Explore the Samaria Gorge

The Samaria Gorge, which is tucked away on the gorgeous island of Crete, is a must-see for any nature lovers traveling to Greece. Although the gorge is 16 kilometers long, some sections are only 4 meters broad. The gorge offers a variety of treks, but it can take up to seven hours to walk the entire area.

Dip your toes in pristine blue water (Mykonos)

In Mykonos, there are numerous beaches where you may take in the azure Aegean Sea waves. If you're staying in the Old Port area, check out the Choras Mikonou little stretch of beach or take a stroll to the close-by Megali Ammos. Psarou, Kalafatis, Paradise, Super Paradise, Agios Stefanos, and Ornos are a few of the island's other well-known beaches.

Discover the Acropolis Museum

The Acropolis Museum, which opened its doors in 2009, is one of Athens' most well-liked contemporary attractions. The structure, which holds some of the most famous antiques in Greece, is composed of cutting-edge glass and steel, so you will recognize it when you see it. The Moschophoros, a figure of a man carrying a calf on his shoulders, and the Parthenon Marbles are a couple of the museum's iconic items. The museum's cafe, which boasts a terrace with views of the magnificent Acropolis, is also well-known.

Marvel at the Epidaurus Theater

The Epidaurus Theater, a place of worship for the well-known god of medicine Asclepius, is located in Epidaurus, a city in the area of Argolis. You can visit the theater and the Sanctuary of Asclepius simultaneously because they are near to each other. You may sit in the stone tiers of the theater, which goes back to the fourth century, and picture witnessing a show there in earlier times.

175

See the birthplace of the Olympic Games (Olympia)

The ancient games were held in Olympia, but the first modern Olympic Games were staged in Athens in 1896. The archaeological site of Olympia, which is now recognized by UNESCO as a World Heritage Site, dates back to the 10th century B.C., and it is filled with remains, including the temple of Zeus and former athletic training grounds.

Visit the monasteries of Meteora

Monasteries perched on soaring rock formations are what Meteora is famous for. Eastern Orthodox monks who were living in the area were forced to flee to Meteora by the Turkish army invasion. Meteora is one of the most impressive religious places in Greece, even though there are only 6 monasteries there, there once would have been around 20. With its abundance of massive boulders and monolithic pillars, Meteora is also a UNESCO World Heritage Site. The rock formations here provide one of Europe's most eerie and breathtaking panoramas.

Admire Hephaestus Temple

The Hephaestus Temple is situated in Athens' lovely Thissio area. This temple is devoted to the gods, as are other Greek temples; in this case, the gods of fire Hephaestus, and Athena, the goddess of antiquity's arts and crafts. On top of Agoreao Koronos Hill, the temple, which is 450 BC old, is located. Hephaestus Temple was built by the same architect who worked on the Pantheon and is renowned for its lovely columns and Pentelic and Parian marble decorations. The structure, which is regarded as one of the most significant in Greek history, is also dotted with friezes and statues.

Explore the history mentioned in "The Iliad" and "The Odyssey" (Mycenae)

Visit the ancient ruins of Mycenae, where legend has it that King Agamemnon once reigned if you want to learn more about the history of the Trojan War and the works of Homer. Admire the structures built in the second century B.C. as you pass through the Lion Gate, the main entryway flanked by lion statues.

Go spelunking at Melissani Cave

Melissani Cave, a rocky cave recognized for its beauty, is located close to Karavomilo. The nearly 4-kilometer-long cave was created over millennia by water eroding the brittle rocks. The equally well-known Melissani Lake, a subterranean body of water that was found in 1951, is located inside the cave. The cave's namesake, the Nymph Melissani, was worshipped there in ancient times.

Learn about olive oil production (Crete)

The largest island in Greece, Crete, is home to various plantations and mills that produce extra virgin olive oil. Cretan Olive Oil Farm offers a hands-on olive oil-making experience, as well as other activities like cheese-making classes and cookery lessons. Paraschakis Family Olive Oil and Lyrakis Family Cretan Company offer factory tours and olive oil goods.

Swim along a lunar-like beach (Milos)

The beach of Sarakiniko on Milos Island is known as Moon Beach, and it is simple to understand why given its curving structure and chalky-white crater surface.

Marvel at the Corinth Canal

The Corinth Canal is one of Greece's most magnificent engineering accomplishments. Construction on it began under the ancient Roman emperor Nero and continued for centuries before being completed in the 19th century by the French. The 6 km long canal has sides that rise to 90 meters, and it is carved out of a chunk of rock. If you are here at the correct moment, you may be able to see ships moving through the canal since it is still in good condition.

Learn some history at the Archaeological Museum of Thessaloniki

The Archaeological Museum of Thessaloniki, which is run by the Ministry of Culture, should not be missed if you find yourself in Thessaloniki. The 1962-built structure in which it is housed is both a superb example of Greek new architecture and a modern Greek gem in and of itself.

Artifacts from Macedonia, a prehistoric Greek culture, can be found at the museum.

Visit a Blue Zone Island where locals enjoy long lives (Ikaria)

Ikaria is a little but formidable island, as evidenced by its Blue Zone designation, which claims that Ikarians live longer than the majority of people worldwide. Adopt a Mediterranean diet (the island's goat cheese and honey are a must), attend a wellness retreat, take naps on Messakti Beach, and generally follow the residents' lead.

Explore the Palace of Malia

The Palace of Malia in Malia was originally erected in 1900 BC, but it has since undergone multiple reconstructions as a result of various natural disasters, including earthquakes. There are many display halls here, together with photo galleries and scale replicas of how the building might have appeared in the past. Keep an eye out for some of its iconic items, including the disk-shaped Kernos Stone, which has 24 holes in it.

Go on a hiking quest (Corfu)

Since Corfu is the second largest island in the Ionian, there are a lot of uncharted territories to discover. The Corfu Trail is a long-distance path that leads walkers across a variety of the island's environments. The entire 111 miles can be hiked if you have many days available, but if not, you can start the trail wherever it is nearest to you.

Have your own 'Mamma Mia!' adventure (Skopelos)

It only takes a ferry voyage to embark on your own Meryl Streep-inspired adventure; "Mamma Mia!" was filmed on the tiny island of Skopelos. Visit the capital's cathedrals, castles, and monasteries, explore Mount Delfi's forest, and pay a visit to the chapel of Agios Ioannis, which Meryl Streep dashes to after the scene from "The Winner Takes It All," in addition to the island's beautiful beaches.

Enjoy the myths and legends at Ancient Mycenae

The Iliad and the Odyssey made Mycenae famous, and it is now a UNESCO World Heritage Site. Mycenae, according to Homer, belonged to the Royal House of Atreus and was constructed by Perseus, a son of Zeus and Danae. Regardless of the truth, Mycenae has established in the sixth century BC, and among its notable features are the imposing Lion Gate and the royal cemetery. Along with lesser homes that once held renowned antiquities like the Warrior Vase, you will also find the Agamemnon Palace and the Great Court.

Visit the ancient site of Phaestos

With breathtaking views of the Messara Plain and Mount Psiloritis, Phaestos, which is around 60 kilometers from Iralkio, is a must-visit location. The palace in Phaestos is comparable to Knossos, and the city is now in ruins. The main draw of this location is the city's continued condition of mostly total ruin, which gives it an otherworldly allure. You can also find some lovely frescoes here. The theater, the main palace structures, the storerooms, and even the crypt can all be explored on the expansive site, which is one giant history lesson.

Dine on the island where the Greek cookbook was invented (Sifnos)

The first Greek cookbook, written by Nicholas Tselementes, was originally published in Sifnos in the early 1900s, and the Cyclades island continues to place a strong emphasis on food. Eat your way through Sifnos by saving recipes for revithada (chickpea stew), lamb mastelo (slow-cooked braised lamb), revithokeftedes (fried chickpea balls), and melopita (honey pie) for dessert.

Bathe in natural hot springs (Euboea)

Take a plunge in the natural hot springs to emulate the ancient Greeks. One of Greece's most well-known spa towns, Edipsos, is located on the island of Euboea, or Evia. People go from far and wide to Edipsos in search of the hot springs' reputed therapeutic properties.

Visit the Vergina Royal Tombs Museum

In Macedonia, the Vergina Royal Tombs Museum is a must-see if you're in the vicinity since you can explore the tumulus, or ancient burial mounds, as well as the underground royal tombs.

The most notable feature of this location is the tomb of Phillip II, which dates to 336 BC. You can also see the artifacts that Phillip II was buried with to prepare for the afterlife, such as a suit of armor, silver chalices, and a shield made of gold and ivory.

Learn some history at the Museum of the Kalavryta Holocaust

This museum, which is also the sole Holocaust Museum in Greece, should not be missed if you happen to be in Kalavryta. The museum is intended to pay tribute to the citizens of this community who suffered attacks by the Nazis during World War II and were slain as a result.

The museum is housed in a former school, where a large number of locals perished. Here, you can find galleries filled with the victims' personal effects as well as old photos of Kalavryta.

Piraeus: An Ancient Harbor, Modern Port, and Ferry Terminus

Piraeus, Greece's biggest modern port, has a more than 2,000-year history. Themistocles built the fortified port as a commercial harbor for Athens in the fifth century BC (12 kilometers away).

Since Piraeus serves as the launching point for vessels bound for Europe and the Near East, it is still Athens' principal commercial port and one of the busiest seaports in the Mediterranean. The Central Port at Piraeus, which serves as the departure point for ferries to all of the Aegean Islands, is where tourists who plan to take a tour of the Greek Islands will almost certainly start their journey.

Mount Parnitha

Mount Parnitha in Central Greece offers a beautiful getaway to nature and is only 40 kilometers (or roughly an hour's drive) from the center of Athens. Visitors who want to breathe in the clean air and take in the pristine splendor of refreshing pine trees flock to this wonderful location.

Drive from Achárnes, an outlying suburb of Athens, to Mount Parnitha National Park. The picturesque road curves sharply as it ascends the mountain. At 900 meters above sea level, Mount Parnitha is the highest mountain peak in Greece. Its magnificent hiking trails wind through heavily forested terrain.

Kaisariani Monastery

One of the most serene and tranquil locations you can visit from Athens is this 11th-century church, not just for its lovely courtyard with sparkling spring water coming from a ram's head, but also for its genuinely breathtaking and placid surroundings.

The Forest Park region is dotted with cypress trees, shrubs, and Mediterranean flowers, making it the perfect location for introspection and clarity.

After seeing the monastery, you can spend some time roaming through the varied hues of Greece's natural environment because the park also features a botanical garden with native Greek plants.

Nemea

Nemea, Athens' wine region, boasts age-old techniques that give the wine a unique flavor. Nemea is a must-visit for wine aficionados.

The scenery is stunning and charmingly Mediterranean, as you might anticipate from a region known for its wine.

Go to a stadium where the Nemean Games were just revived after being staged there for centuries during your visit.

The Temple of Apollo

An archaeological site is located 300 kilometers from Athens, making it one of the longest trips you can do. A few kilometers from the town of Thermos, the Temple of Apollo is situated in an improbably beautiful setting on the banks of Lake Trichonis. The temple is a tribute to the architectural skill of the builders of the period as well as to the devotion of the devotees of the Sun God Apollo.

The Monastery of Dafní

The Monastery of Dawn, which is a UNESCO World Heritage Site and is only 10 kilometers from the heart of Athens, was first a pagan sanctuary before being transformed into a Christian monastery and finally into the current monastery in 1080.

The structure is a must-see for its breathtakingly intricate interior decorations, which contain mosaics from the 11th Century and give it the reputation of being one of the most stunning Byzantine churches in Greece.

Hydra Island

A quick 2-hour trip from Piraeus Port in Athens will take you to a gorgeously rural island that makes for a truly lovely getaway from the city. People from all walks of life, including artists, travelers, and foodies, are drawn to Hydra Island because it forbids the use of any form of motorcycle or car Because of this, it is a delightfully irresistible day trip to explore the urban streets of rustic buildings carved into the numerous hillsides. Prepare for a lovely day of exploring Hydra Island to locate your ideal pastime. The island offers it all, including deserted churches and remote beaches.

Attic Riviera (Coast of Apollo)

If you're looking for something a little different than temples and historical ruins, you could visit the Coast of Apollo, a stunning stretch of coastline that runs between Athens and Cape Sounion and has a variety of attractions to offer aside from the typical ancient landmarks.

As you go along the coast, you will come across a wide selection of golf courses, stunning beaches, and marinas that are home to opulent ships and sailing clubs.

Go out and enjoy some of life's nicer things by traveling to the Riviera's sun-kissed stretches.

CHAPTER SEVEN
Nightlife in Greece & the islands

Greece and the Greek islands are renowned throughout the world for their vibrant nightlife and romantic date nights.

Greece has a large number of taverns and clubs.

Greece's nightlife is a significant part of the nation's culture.

A night out typically begins with dinner at one of the many pubs or restaurants and continues with a soft drink in a lounge bar or magnificent nightclubs with wild parties until morning.

The most famous locations for the party are:

• Athens • Mykonos • Ios • Paros • Rhodes • Kos • Heraklion • Zante

Bars & Pubs

Greece has a large number of late-night bars that play a variety of music, including Greek and international pop, alternative rock, jazz, Latin, and much more.

Even in the most remote areas of Greek islands, these bars can be discovered.

In Greece, a lot of coffee shops start as pubs in the evening. They typically stay open until 2 or 3 a.m., depending on the number of customers, and serve any type of drink outside beneath the stars. These pubs are the focal point of the nightlife on many Greek islands.

Night Clubs

Nightclubs can be found in numerous locations in Greece because the nightlife is a common aspect of many people's daily lives there. They start operating at around midnight and remain open until around 6 or 7 a.m.

Many of these Greek island clubs, especially those in Mykonos, Paros, Ios, Crete, Rhodes, Kos, and other well-known locations, attract well-known DJs from around the globe to spin their music.

In clubs, there is an abundance of booze, and everyone is thirsty for fun and celebration.

Best Greek Party Islands

Mykonos

Mykonos is frequently referred to as the "Ibiza of Greece," and at night, its cool, cosmopolitan atmosphere transforms into a hedonistic party paradise.

The island, dubbed the best destination in Greece for nightlife, is home to Paradise Club, one of the most well-known clubs in Europe with three stages and its very own swimming pool, as well as some of the biggest party nights in the Aegean.

There are numerous things to do in Mykonos once the hangover has passed. Alternatively, you may just relax and take in some of the world's most stunning beaches.

The best nightlife in Greece can be experienced on this party island hopping tour.

Rhodes

Rhodes is a party island with something to offer everyone that is both multicultural and distinctly Greek.

While some of the best clubs and discos are dispersed around Rhodes Town, Faliraki's well-known resort offers bustling clubs and bars full of revelers on booze cruises all year long.

Both Bar Street and Club Street provide precisely what is described on the label and are packed with tourists during the summer.

Ios

You won't be let down when you find this hidden gem, which has some of Greece's wildest clubs, including Aftershock, Disco 69, Blue Note, and Scorpion. The renowned Far Out Beach Club, where you may party all day and night, is located on Mylopotas Beach.

Stay in July and you could get the chance to attend one of the amazing Full Moon Parties that are held on the island, where you can party beneath the stars and watch the sunrise in this idyllic paradise.

Santorini

Santorini may appear idyllic and serene, which it is in some parts, but it also knows how to throw a party. Enjoy a cocktail at one of the many beachside bars or get glammed up at one of the ultra-hip club nights hosted by some of the biggest names in the DJ industry.

If you prefer a more laid-back lifestyle, there are many cool, eclectic clubs and beach bars that play jazz, Latin, and soul music all night long.

Corfu

Corfu isn't out of the running when it comes to party spots. The island's high student population helps it maintain its standing as one of the most well-liked tourist attractions in Greece year after year.

Visit the vibrant pubs and hip clubs on the Kavos and Ipsos strip, or chill out at trendy beach bars in Kontokali or Sidari. All year long, Corfu boasts a vibrant and energetic party culture with everything from paint parties to powder parties to party nights at the zoo.

Kos

Kos is renowned for its enormous variety of venues to accommodate all interests and budgets, whether you are searching for intense EDM, laid-back jazz and Latin, or modern pop. Kos Town has some of the most renowned bars on the Island and is varied and vibrant.

Get on it with the locals in any of the neighborhood bars and taverns hid away in the old streets, or mingle with the gorgeous people in the famous Sky Bar. Check out the resort of Kardamena, which hosts several bar crawls and package holidays, if you want all-night partying for the more intense.

Paros

Paros is the destination for you if you're looking for some planned amusement. There are numerous beach bars, lounge bars, nightclubs, and beach parties to choose from in the villages of Naoussa and Parikia.

You can pretty much guarantee that this island gets chaotic during the busy season because it is very well-liked by university students from all over the world.

Get your Aussie drinking heads on because the island has a wonderfully hedonistic ambiance that ranges from hippie beach shack pubs to posh cosmopolitan resort resorts.

Zakynthos

Laganas, Tsilivi, and Agassi are excellent locations for a wild night of partying. As a well-liked package vacation location, there is a ton of planned entertainment available at the resorts.

There is always something happening in Zakynthos, from bar crawls to boat parties, themed nights, and pool parties. The island has stunning beaches with relaxed beach bars where you can unwind after a long night out.

Crete

Malia is right there with the legendary Ibiza as one of the largest party destinations in all of Europe.

Crete is a destination for anyone wishing to party hard this summer, with its abundance of gorgeous beaches, clear waters, and some of the busiest and greatest club nights in all of Greece.

Aside from the amazing pubs and clubs like HELP Bar, Bikini Beach, or the renowned Camelot Castle that are available, the island frequently hosts booze cruises, boat parties, paint parties, and even full-moon parties.

Thessaloniki

Despite not being an island, this city is nevertheless deserving of recognition as a great place to party. Thessaloniki is well-liked by jet-set Europeans and mainland Greeks during the summer due to its diverse music culture and nightclubs that are tucked away in former industrial locations.

It is a well-known party staple for travelers around the world, with everything from live rock concerts to hard-core dance nights. Even better, you may put your bets at one of Europe's most luxurious casinos or take in some of Greece's best Bouzouki entertainment.

Best Night Clubs in Greece

Paradise Beach Club

The founding of Paradise in 1969 signaled the beginning of a culture, and it quickly gained notoriety as one of the top clubs in the nation.

Located on the Paradise coast, a place where you may savor the simple pleasures of life with pristine waters, a warm sun, and sparkling dunes. It is without a doubt hidden heaven where people have gathered to seek out fantastic music, camaraderie, and pleasure. At this stunning location on the Mediterranean, the most well-known local and international DJs have spun their tunes and staged some of the most unforgettable nights.

Opened From April through October, the paradise beach club is open and offers day and nighttime activities as well as lodging at various price points so you can essentially wake up to the party.

The Clumsies

The bar, which consistently ranks among the top bars not just in Greece but also around the world, is essential to Athens' nightlife. If you want to maintain a fashionable culture, it is the perfect location.

The 1919 building's restorations, in which the proprietors accomplished a beautiful balancing act between the old and the new, are what ultimately lend The Clumsies its irresistible appeal.

For the third year in a row, The Clumsies was included by Drinks International Magazine as one of the top 50 bars in the world on the top 10 list for both 2016 and 2017. Other well-known bars also made the list.

New York Beach Club

The New York Beach Club has been one of the most renowned clubs in the nation since it opened 30 years ago and offers the best party atmosphere and unforgettable nights for both locals and visitors.

This club, which offers a view of the limitless sea and is the best sailing destination for your Greek adventure, is located in the center of Hersonissos on the major beach road. It is driven by constant invention and innovation.

This club offers outstanding services, premium drinks, food, music for every taste, and an unforgettable experience for you and your friends. It also has cooperative management and accessible staff available twenty-four hours a day.

Cavo Paradiso

Cavo Paradiso is without a doubt the most well-known club on the island of Mykonos and has earned legendary status in the global party scene for having hosted some of the most notable occasions there. The music industry, its performers, and clubgoers worldwide all cite the club as one of the greatest music & entertainment venues on the planet. On annual club lists released by foreign media, it consistently holds a high position.

As the sun slowly descends over the horizon, bidding farewell to a memorable night, it beautifully embraces the surrounding natural splendor to create an extraordinary ambiance where you may dance until the early hours to the best music.

Void

The biggest summer debut in Chora's nightlife is Void, probably one of the biggest and best clubs in Mykonos and Greece. It has a reputation that most clubs fail to obtain after years of operation.

The Void hosts world-famous DJs to enjoy the best parties on the island in a setting of outstanding architecture and amazing people, creating a setting unlike any other. Void's minimalist architecture acknowledges its Greek heritage.

Enigma

The unique and vibrant capital of Santorini Island, Fira, is where Enigma Club is situated. It is only 50 meters from the main plaza.

Enigma, a popular nightclub that has been around since it first opened in 1979, is one of the greatest places to spend your evenings while sipping delicious drinks and dancing to the best music. Its hip atmosphere ensures that you'll have a fantastic time with friends who become family.

In addition, The Enigma's party planners offer custom parties that are organized to perfection and meet all of your requirements. Travelers' favorite tropical locations are sure to become the enigma bars, which serve the greatest cocktails in the area.

Scandinavian Bar & Disco

The Scandinavian Bar has been a mainstay of the Mykonos nightlife for almost 40 years. Your nights in Mykonos will be genuinely fantastic thanks to a wide variety of superb cocktails and beverages and a wonderful music playlist provided by well-known local and national DJs.

They have established themselves as the leading nightclub on Mykonos by providing a warm environment and top-notch service from Monday through Sunday.

The majority of the people who frequent the bar are young, and the dance floor is crowded and fun. Here, drinks, dancing, and music will make your night. For a private party, bottle service is also offered. Prepare yourself to experience some of the most inexpensive cocktails in the city with the best people.

Sodade2

Sodade2, a downtown Athens nightclub that has been largely attracting LGBTQ patrons, is situated in the city's cultural hub, Kerameikos, and is one of the adaptable most and exciting homosexual clubs in the city.

At Sodade2, three separate party spaces are available: the main dance floor, a second dance floor, and a nearby terrace.

The top DJs in town are in charge of each space, which features a different kind of music and gives each patron a special nightclub experience.

Many different musical genres are available at Sodade2. Alternatives abound and include pop, house, jazz, disco, and electro beats, as well as beats from other genres including rock and jazz.

Sodae2 is one of the top gay clubs in the nation, offering amazing events and memorable experiences.

Best Nightclubs in Athens

- Bogart
- Booze
- Clown Dogs
- Lohan Nightclub
- Toy Room Club
- Dybbuk Athens Nightclub
- Boiler Room
- Syntagma
- Steam

Best clubs in Santorini

- Koo Club Santorini
- STOA SANTORINI
- Casablanca Soul Santorini
- Aion Cocktail Bar
- Mamounia Club Santorini
- Erotokritos
- Tango Santorini
- Two Brothers Bar Santorini

Best beach clubs in Mykonos

- Nammos Mykonos
- Principote Mykonos
- Paradise Beach Club
- Jackie 'O beach club
- Scorpios
- SantAnna Mykonos

CHAPTER EIGHT
Famous Dishes to Try in Greece

Taramasalata

Greek food isn't complete without traditional dips like tzatziki (yogurt, cucumber, and garlic), melitzanosalata (aubergine), and fava (creamy split pea purée). However, the delicious fish roe dip, taramasalata, must be tried. With either a drizzle of extra virgin olive oil or a squeeze of lemon, this creamy mixture of pink or white fish roe, with a potato or bread basis, tastes the finest.

Olives and olive oil

Greeks have been growing olives for thousands of years; some even claim that Athena bestowed an olive tree upon the city of Athens to win the city's favor. Local olives, some of which are cured in a hearty sea salt brine, are served with Greek meals, while others, like wrinkled throubes, are eaten straight from the tree uncured. Similar to how it is used extensively in cooking and salads, olive oil is also drizzled over most dips and foods. It is known as the "elixir of Greece."

Dolmades

Every region and every home in Greece has its take on dolmades, whether it's the traditional vine leaf parcel or veggies like tomatoes, peppers, and courgettes that have been hollowed out, stuffed, and baked. Long-grain rice and minced beef are frequently used in the filling. Vegetarian variations of the dish feature rice that has been infused with flavorful blends of thyme, dill, fennel, and oregano. Another option is to use pine nuts.

Moussaka

There are many moussaka variations throughout the Mediterranean and the Balkans, but the traditional Greek oven-bake is composed of layers of sautéed aubergine, minced lamb, fried puréed tomato, onion, garlic, and spices like cinnamon and allspice, a small amount of potato, and a final creamy topping of béchamel sauce and cheese.

Grilled meat

Greeks are experts at roasting and grilling meat over charcoal. Greece's favorite fast food is still souvlaki, which is chunks of skewered pork served on pita bread with plenty of tzatziki and chopped tomatoes and onions. The same method is frequently used to serve gyros. Local free-range lamb and hog are the most popular meats in the taverna, but the young goat is also a crowd favorite.

Fresh fish

Sit down in a tavern by the sea and eat as the people have done since ancient times. Fresh fish and calamari from the Mediterranean and Aegean Seas are delicious and prepared with the least amount of bother by being grilled whole and drizzled with avgolemono (a lemon and oil dressing). Barbouni (red mullet) and marida (whitebait), two flavorful smaller fish, are best lightly cooked.

Courgette balls (kolokythokeftedes)

Try these appetizers whenever you have the chance. They can be a patty or a gently cooked ball. Typically, the fritter is created with grated or puréed courgette mixed with dill, mint, or other top-secret spice blends. You simply can't go wrong when served with tzatziki because of its reviving coolness.

Octopus

Octopus is one of the most recognizable sights of Greece; it is dried out along harbors like laundry. They are delicious as an appetizer on the grill or marinated as a major dish for wine-stew dishes.

Feta & other cheeses

Fresh cheese is a delight in Greece. For creamy, exquisite feta that is preserved in large brine barrels, ask behind-the-market counters (nothing like the type that comes in plastic tubs in markets outside of Greece). Or, try graviera, a firm, golden-white cheese that is excellent cubed or fried as saganaki. In bakeries, you may find tyropita (cheese pie), while in tavernas, you can order salads like Cretan dakos, which is topped with crumbled mizithra, a soft white cheese.

Honey & baklava

Greeks adore sweets, which are frequently made with honey and olive oil and wrapped in flaky filo pastry. Honey, filo, and crushed nuts are components of traditional baklava. Or try galaktoboureko, a delicious pastry packed with custard. Local thyme honey sprinkled over fresh, thick Greek yogurt is a simpler dessert.

Best Restaurants in Greece

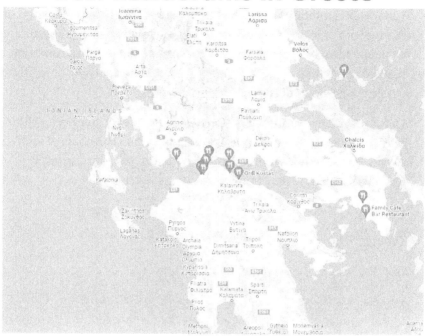

Ambrosia Restaurant, Santorini

Ambrosia Restaurant is one of Greece's most well-known and picturesque fine dining establishments. It is located in Oia, on the Caldera coast of Santorini, inside a Cycladic mansion, and has white tablecloths.

The most romantic date night of your life can be had at this fine dining establishment, which has a stunning view of the Aegean Sea.

Ambrosia offers alternatives for seafood, meat including lamb, duck, and veal, crisp fresh salads, mouthwatering pasta, and sweets on its small menu, which is made up of specialty dishes.

Address: Cliffside Terrace at Village Center, Oía 847 02, Greece

Timings: 6:30 PM to 11:30 PM

Tudor Hall is a showcase of excellent dining in luxury and is located on the seventh story of the renowned King George Hotel. This restaurant would be ideal to visit for lunch or dinner to experience the amazing sight of the Acropolis in all its splendor. The outside dining area offers breathtaking views of the old city of Athens.

Tudor Hall delivers some of the best gourmet treats in Athens, with a modern touch on Greek food, including salads, meats coupled with good wines, and decadent patisserie desserts. There are several vegetarian alternatives at this restaurant as well.

Address: Vasileos Georgiou A 3, Athina 105 64, Greece

Timings: 6:30 AM to 1:30 PM, 6 PM to 2 AM

Peskesi, Crete

Peskesi, a restaurant serving specialties from Cretan cuisine in the Cretan capital of Heraklion, celebrates the Cretan tradition through its rustic-chic setting and cuisine. You may be sure that at this hidden gem, you will have a genuine Greek farm-to-table experience because of the establishment's core values of sustainable agriculture and gastronomy.

With dishes like the renowned Dakos, distinctive Cretan wines, cheesecake, baklava, and slow-cooked goat, it is understandable why this restaurant is so well-liked. Make sure to reserve a seat at this table well in advance.

Address: Kapetan Charalampi 6-8, Herkelion, Iraklio 712 02, Greece

Timings: 1 PM to 2 AM

A superb luxury hotel with a variety of dining alternatives is the Four Seasons Astir Palace Resort in Athens. Their Michelin-starred Mediterranean restaurant Pelagos is a spectacular fine dining experience for all gourmet cuisine connoisseurs.

Visit the exquisite Mercato Italian restaurant at Astir Palace Resort for a delectable meal.

Address: Apollonos 40, Vouliagmeni 166 71, Greece

Timings: 7 PM to 10 PM

Merastri, Crete

Merastri, a renowned and award-winning Cretan restaurant in Heraklion, Crete, is another traditional eatery that features components of traditional Greek food. Merastri offers a wide variety of foods that are prepared in a wood oven while sticking with tradition.

Visit this restaurant to sample the components of their sizable grilled meat platter, particularly their grilled lamb that is baked with potatoes in a wood oven.

They also serve various specialties that are very well-liked by customers, such as filled zucchini flowers, goat's cheese salad, spaghetti, and zucchini balls. One of the best locations to unwind and nourish your spirit is unquestionably here.

Address: Chrisostomou 17, Iraklio 713 06, Greece

Timings: 6 PM to 12 AM

Maiandros Restarant, Athens

In the hubbub of central Athens is a casual eating establishment serving outstanding traditional Greek and Mediterranean cuisine. Maiandros offers a stunning perspective of the ancient city and is one of the most authentic places to discover simple local comfort food in all of Athens.

Greek-style coffee establishment Maiandros offers delicious meals and fantastic drinks. This is one of the best Greece restaurants for affordable eats, offering a welcoming ambiance and delectable specialties including beef and orzo pasta, grilled lamb, and chicken souvlaki.

Address: Adrianou 47, Athina 105 55, Greece

Timings: 10:30 AM to 12 AM

Alficon Speakeasy Gastronomy, Athens

The Alficon Speakeasy is a charming Michelin-star-holding restaurant in Athens that provides a great dining culinary experience. The expertly curated degustation menus at Alficon are true works of art that you can eat.

Address: Ironda 8, Athina 116 35, Greece

Timings: 7 PM to 12 AM (Closed on Mondays)

Fokos Taverna, Mykonos

The Fokos Taverna, a quaint, laid-back eatery with stunning views of the Aegean Sea located on Mykonos' beach, has a gorgeously rustic, traditional Greek feel. Traditional, straightforward cuisine that is soulful and genuine is served.

Enjoy some delicious beers and their lamb chops, Greek salad, Caesar salad, shrimp in sauce, and other delectable salads while unwinding and relaxing on a lazy afternoon. With hearty Greek food and a stunning sea view, you can't go wrong at all.

Address: Fokos Φωκός, Ano Mera 846 00, Greece

Timings: 1 PM to 7 PM

Spondi, Athens

Spondi in Athens, the only two-Michelin star restaurant in Greece, is a place to indulge, taste, and enjoy food in a completely new way. The chef at this restaurant, which serves modern French and Mediterranean cuisine, is renowned for curating their Discovery Menu, a 9-course degustation.

This dinner, which includes fish, meat, scallops, and foie gras, may be expensive but it's an experience you won't soon forget. This gourmet dining establishment requires a reservation.

Address: Pirronos 5, Athina 116 36, Greece

Timings: 7:30 PM to 11:15 PM

Avli Restaurant, Crete

The best restaurant in Crete is Avli Restaurant, also known as "A," which is situated in Heraklion and is known for serving up the best traditional comfort food in Greece. It uses only the freshest meat, cheese, and veggies.

This family-run establishment offers a genuinely soulful experience, and the owners take great care and interest in describing the menu items to the customers in English.

The gastronomic journey via flavors and taste that Avli puts you on includes delectable mezze platters, fresh salads, seductive appetizers, and perfectly prepared meat and seafood entrees. It has a particular flavor profile that is Mediterranean and is great with fine wine, sharp ouzo, or light, delicious tsipouro.

Address: Smirnis 31, Iraklio 713 03, Greece

Timings: 1:30 PM to 1 AM

CHAPTER NINE
Greece Travel Tips

Ferries vs. Catamarans

Greece has year-round great weather with plenty of sunshine. Summers can be sweltering hot, while winters are typically brief. But the sea has its laws. Strong winds are continually present on most islands, and you never know when the sea may be choppy. Even in the summer, when it might seem that the sea would be calm, the winds can be very strong. Your trip plans may be impacted by the 'Meltemi,' a powerful northern wind that appears from June through September.

The Beaufort wind force scale is always used by Greeks to gauge wind speed. Thus, it serves as the foundation for every local weather forecast. It's a useful resource for tourists going to Greece so they may prepare for their trip to the Greek islands. Large waves can cause some passengers to feel anxious and queasy while they are traveling by sea, which is not frequently stopped (except in extreme gales).

Remember to Bring Cash

In Greece, money is king. Even though credit cards are accepted everywhere in Greece, locals favor using cash. Cards appear to be taboo, especially with the older generation. The majority of Greeks prefer to pay in cash, and following a long decade of a financial crisis, the population appears to be even less trusting of credit cards. Although the Greek government encourages card payments to prevent tax evasion, the truth is that if given the option, locals will always opt for cash.

There are more factors at play here than just the decisions made by the Greek government. For instance, in remote locations, POS devices won't be able to connect to the Internet easily.

While traveling on tiny islands like Donoussa or Anafi, you might encounter this difficulty more than once. Furthermore, the lack of banks in such locations—which can be found on the Greek mainland—is another reason to carry cash.

Even though there are ATMs on most islands, you can't always trust them to have enough cash on hand to meet your needs. An ATM running out of cash won't make the news, especially during the summer when many people travel to the most popular tourist destinations. However, it still occurs—and frequently.

It's preferable to bring enough cash with you and attempt to use a card whenever you want to pay than to bring nothing at all and rely on an Internet connection to use a POS or to wait for the ATM to replenish itself.

Using a Taxi App is Better

If a local is operating a taxi in a remote area (on an island or the mainland), finding one won't be a problem. You can get the taxi driver's phone number from your hotel, especially on the smaller islands, and call them whenever you want.

In contrast, there will be a huge supply of taxis in places like Athens or Thessaloniki. Greek taxi drivers used to have a bad reputation for overcharging tourists. These incidents continue, even though the situation has improved over the past ten years. Installing the Beat app on your smartphone is your best option for getting reasonable prices and moving around with ease.

Since Uber was outlawed in Greece a few years ago, your best bet is to use a taxi app. It functions essentially the same as every other taxi app you may have on your phone. Simply turn on your GPS, allow the app to find you, and enter your destination. If the estimated price sounds reasonable to you, you can order your taxi using the app. You can give your driver feedback once you've reached your destination.

216

Finally, you have the option of paying with cash or a credit card. You can select it in advance, and you can board and exit taxis if you save the card in the app.

Book in Advance

Every year, Greece draws a huge number of visitors. Greece welcomed 34 million tourists in 2019, a record number for the country's tourism sector. That's therefore nearly 3,5 times the population of Greece, to give you a better idea. You can now get a good idea of how crowded it can be in specific locations like Santorini by taking into account the fact that the majority of people visit particular locations across the nation.

The shoulder months saw a lot of bookings in recent years, despite the high season selling out quickly. The best travel advice for Greece is to make all of your reservations in advance. Starting to plan and reserve everything, including flights, hotels, and ferries, should be done once you know your precise dates.

You'll not only get some great deals, but you'll also have the tranquility needed for a restful vacation. Therefore, it is always preferable to make all of your reservations in advance if you intend to visit Greece between April and October.

The opening hours fluctuate

Greece is no different from any other nation in having regulations governing store hours. As a result of the erratic schedule, it is preferable to make a direct purchase if you are in Greece and come across something you like or need.

To begin with, Sundays are a day when all stores remain closed. The majority of the time, Sundays don't have open shops, though that does happen occasionally. In comparison to malls or large chain stores like H&M, smaller shops typically operate on different schedules. Particularly, on Mondays and Wednesdays, most small shops close at 3 o'clock. The large chains, on the other hand, are open until 9 PM.

Avoid Flushing Toilet Paper in Greece

This is a useful tip for traveling and a basic thing to understand before going to Greece. You won't be allowed to flush toilet paper in any Greek home or hotel, according to the locals. Instead, they will politely ask you to use the trashcan. The Pericles-era sewage system does not exist in Greece today. Simply put, Greece's sewage pipes are very small due to a variety of factors. They have a diameter of only 50 mm, which prevents toilet paper from passing through. You should always keep this in mind because using toilet paper can damage the pipes, which is something you must prevent.

You won't experience any cleanliness problems while you're there because Greeks take great care to empty the trash cans each day. Just keep in mind that you shouldn't flush toilet paper whenever you use a restroom, whether it's in a house, a restaurant, or a hotel. Most of the time, it will also be noted on a sticker in Greek and English.

The sunshade is your ally

Always carry sunscreen when traveling in Greece. You can purchase one from your home or a local retailer. It is advised to carry sunscreen with you because the sun is particularly strong during the summer. If you go to Greece in the fall, don't undervalue the sun. The sun is still very bright in most places, especially on the islands.

Proper Clothes Selection

Except at a few designated beaches, nudity is strongly discouraged. You should take caution when choosing what to wear. It is best not to wear short, skimpy shorts or tops when visiting churches or monasteries. When you are here, you will need to cover up a bit more. This is the outcome of the older generation's deeply ingrained conservatism, which is still prevalent in many places. However, there are some beaches and locations where you are free to dress however you, please.

How to save money on your Greek island adventure

To explore the island at your own pace, rent a car

Renting a car is one of the finest methods to visit the numerous stunning islands in Greece. Renting a car not only enables you to go at your speed but also enables you to see off-the-beaten-path locations that might not be easily reached by public transportation.

Additionally, renting a car is far less expensive than using cabs or paying for guided excursions while you're on vacation. When traveling with your family, you can save money and make the most of your time by hiring your car and avoiding expensive middlemen like tour operators, especially if you're searching for a genuine and immersive travel experience.

Take advantage of free activities, like swimming and hiding

There are numerous reasons to take advantage of free activities when on a family vacation to any Greek island. For starters, these activities are not only entertaining and interesting, but they may also be a fantastic way to exercise.

You can be sure that the entire family will have a blast whether you decide to go mountain hiking or spend the day swimming in the sea. Additionally, by lowering your overall travel expenses, these free activities might free up more money for the things that matter most to you. The best part is that they make it possible for you to connect with local culture and take in Greece's stunning natural beauty without breaking the bank.

Avoid purchasing tourist traps such as boat tours and donkey rides

Anyone who has ever taken a family holiday to Greece is aware of the abundance of options for tourists to spend their money on tourist traps.

There is no shortage of things to spend your money on, from donkey rides to boat cruises.

However, if you want to make the most of your trip, you must avoid these tourist traps at all costs. They are frequently pricey, overbooked, and fail to accurately portray island life. Save your cash and go island hopping on your terms.

Spend some time exploring the neighborhood and speaking with residents about their customs and way of life.

This will both help you understand Greek culture better and guarantee that your family vacation will be one to remember.

To get the best deals, reserve your flight and lodging well in advance

Every parent is aware of the challenge of balancing the need for convenience and the desire to save money when traveling with children. Kids, after all, have a lot of requirements: they want entertainment during lengthy rides and flights, food options in the hotel room, and activities to keep them occupied. At the same time, everyone wants to travel for a reasonable price, especially if money is limited. Fortunately, planning will enable you to uncover fantastic offers that satisfy both of these requirements for your travel and lodging.

By making your reservations far in advance, you allow yourself plenty of time to check out various hotels and flight possibilities. This entails that you can keep an open mind about your choice of location or particular properties and search for savings or special deals from tour operators or hotel chains.

Ask locals where they like to eat and drink and be open to trying new things

Asking locals for recommendations on where to eat and drink is one of the finest ways to appreciate a new location, as any seasoned traveler will tell you. You can save money by doing this in addition to avoiding tourist traps. It can be expensive to take a family trip, so it can be tempting to try to cut costs by eating at cheap chain restaurants.

CHAPTER TEN
Greece Travel Safety Tips

Crime

In tourist regions and on the islands, pickpocketing and pocketbook theft are becoming more frequent crimes. Passports and other valuables should be left in a secure location rather than being carried on your person. When taking public transportation, exercise extra caution. Pickpocketing and bag snatching are frequent, and criminals may even slash luggage and backpacks to get at the contents.

Although there have only been a few incidents of major physical assaults against visitors, violent crime against them is rare. Avoid walking around the neighborhoods of Monastiraki and Omonia in Athens, as well as in the area of the Larissa and Peloponnese bus and train terminals after nightfall.

Greece has some of the toughest drug prohibitions in all of Europe, and even visitors are subject to heavy penalties. Travelers should abstain from all drug-related activities.

Strikes and Protests

Greek cities commonly see protest gatherings, especially in Athens' main squares. Visitors are advised to pay attention to local media and steer clear of these protests since they could turn violent and because police have used tear gas to disperse people. Similar to how strikes routinely halt rail, maritime, and air travel. For the most recent news, keep an eye on the media and your transportation company, and have a backup plan in place in case your trip is delayed.

Natural disasters

Due to its location in a seismically active area, Greece occasionally experiences earthquakes and volcanic eruptions. During the dry summers, Greece is extremely vulnerable to forest fires (June to

September). In all parts of the nation, floods can happen in the spring and winter. In the event of a natural disaster, heed the advice of local emergency service workers, keep an eye on local media, and get in touch with your consulate or embassy.

Road safety

The riskiest part of traveling in Greece is certainly on the roads. According to Eurostat data, Greece has more road fatalities overall than the norm for other European nations (64 per million inhabitants and 49 per million respectively in 2018). Drivers in Greece frequently exhibit aggressive behavior and bad driving standards; therefore, pedestrians should exercise additional caution when crossing streets. Be aware that many of the country's roads are in poor condition, and roaming animals can be a problem in some areas.

Local medical services

All inhabitants of Greece and members of the European Union (EU) are entitled to free healthcare. Public hospitals can provide free basic emergency care to visitors from outside the EU, but keep in mind that they may be understaffed and out of medical supplies. Private hospitals offer a higher caliber of care, but they are also pricier and sometimes demand upfront payment. Pack sufficient of any prescription medication before traveling to Greece because there have occasionally been shortages in the country's pharmaceutical supply.

Eating and drinking

Greece has strict laws governing food safety, and the tap water there is safe to drink. Though many islanders prefer to drink bottled water, keep in mind that the tap water on the islands may taste different as it is desalinated seawater.

General health dangers

Food-borne illnesses like brucellosis occasionally go into epidemics. Avoid eating raw or undercooked meals, and don't consume unpasteurized dairy products. Heat stroke is a more typical illness-causing factor. Wear lightweight clothing, a hat, sunscreen, and plenty of water throughout the sweltering summer days.